Architectural Guide
Bangkok

Architectural Guide
Bangkok

Edited by Pattaranan Takkanon for
the Association of Siamese Architects
under Royal Patronage

DOM
publishers

asa สมาคมสถาปนิกสยาม ในพระบรมราชูปถัมภ์
The Association of Siamese Architects under Royal Patronage

DON MUEANG
Don Mueang International Airport
SAI MAI
LAK SI
KHLONG SAM WA
BANG KHEN
CHATUCHAK
LAT PHRAO
KHAN NA YAO
BANG SUE
BUENG KUM
WANG THONGLANG
TALING CHAN
BANG PHLAT
DUSIT
PHAYA THAI
DIN DAENG
HUAI KHWANG
SAPHAN SUNG
BANGKOK NOI
PHRA NAKHON
RATCHATHEWI
BANG KAPI
BANGKOK YAI
PATHUM WAN
WATTHANA
PHASI CHAROEN
THONBURI
KHLONG SAN
BANG RAK
SUAN LUANG
SATHON
KHLONG TOEI
BANG KHAE
BANG KHO LAEM
PRAWET
CHOM THONG
YAN NAWA
PHRA KHANONG
BANG BON
RAT BURANA
BANG NA
THUNG KHRU
BANG KHUN THIAN
Chao Phraya
0
10 km
Gulf of Thailand

Contents

The Bangkok Way of Life

What is the first thing that comes to mind when talking about Bangkok, the capital of Thailand? Common answers include the following: a capital with too much traffic on the roads, its delicious cuisine, a city that is divided into two by the Chao Phraya River, the Grand Palace or Wat Phra Sri Rattana Satsadaram (Temple of the Emerald Buddha). The capital certainly has a number of spectacles for visitors to marvel at. It is not an overstatement to say, "Bangkok has everything you could possibly wish to find". The city welcomes everybody with smiles and the art of giving. It is also common for tourists who initially intended to pay a short visit to extend their stay and then soon become permanent residents. Bangkok is thereby not a stop en route, but rather a final destination.

In terms of history, when Ayutthaya lost its independence in 1767 Somdet Phrachao Taksin Maharaj established Thonburi as the new capital between 1767 and 1782. In 1782, King Rama I, the first monarch of the Chakri Dynasty, moved the capital to Bangkok which resulted in wide political, economic, social and cultural changes. The city adapted Western culture into the Thai way of life, as evident in the designs for houses, temples and even palaces. Architecture shifted from simplicity to complexity to depict the social hierarchy. There are many visible influences of different cultures, such as Chinese under the reign of King Rama III and Western under the reign of King Rama IV and King Rama V. These influences are reflected in the traditional Thai style, the applied Thai style and the combination of Western and Eastern architecture with Thai elements. The various types of communities, ways of life and the mixture of skyscrapers, shophouses and slums make the city of Bangkok one of the most unique and enchanting places for travelling in the world.

Metropolises around the world, such as New York, London and Tokyo, share similar traits in that they are covered with concrete jungle, their people are always in a hurry, time is more precious than material possessions, traffic congestion is a serious issue and theft is widespread. Bangkok, however, is a place where the identity of civilisation still remains. This is reflected in the traditional arts, culture, architecture and wideheld beliefs. Every morning, monks can be seen walking barefoot along the street. Buddhist people offer food to them since they believe in

Overview of the Chao Phraya River

good fortune by offering luxuries to their ancestors. Temples are also a centre for Buddhist communities. During important Buddhist events, people will make merit, listen to sermons, pour ceremonial water, offer items to monks, release birds and fish and worship the Erawan Shrine, in addition to other monuments or statues. Although Buddhism is the primary religion, people are free to practise other religions as well. Essentially, all religions co-exist peacefully among Thai people; it is hence a common sight to see temples, churches, mosques and Chinese joss houses all clustered together within the same area.

In terms of sports, flying kites has been a popular activity in Bangkok since the Sukhothai period, in addition to Thai boxing. The latter is a type of martial art which combines all fighting techniques and uses all parts of the body. Thai people and tourists also often schedule a therapeutic Thai massage which uses local herbs to release muscle pains and stress from both body and mind. Classes are taught at Wat Phra Chettuphon Wimon Mangkhlaram Ratchaworamahawihan, or Wat Pho, the first academic school for massage in Thailand. Other tourist attractions include traditional Thai plays, music, dance dramas and performances, such as Lakhon, Khon, Lam-tad and Li-ke, which are performed across a number of art venues. Such venues often depict both traditional and contemporary styles of Thai architecture in their design. In common with Bangkok's way of life and its architecture, food cultures are also shaped by a blend of foreign influences, such as Japanese, Korean, Persian, Chinese and French. Flavours and prices vary. Visitors can find good-quality restaurants of all kinds anywhere, encompassing street vendors, shophouses and even high-end hotels. In fact, food outlets are visible everywhere. Bangkok also has a wide range of shopping centres and markets, such as small local markets, floating markets, weekend markets and vast shopping complexes. Well-known places include the floral market at Pak Khlong Talad, the wholesale clothing market at Bobae, the clothing market aimed for teenagers at Siam Square – offering a number of high-street fashions – and a shopping centre for new technology gadgets at Digital Gateway, situated in the same area. However, the most famous shopping centre, which is targeted at all age groups, is Chatuchak –

the largest weekend market in the world. It provides a number of products sourced from all parts of Thailand. Here there is a wide range of choices available to visitors, while prices are generally cheap.

One of the most famous festivals to take place in Bangkok is Songkran. It is the Thai New Year's festival which Thai people celebrate by pouring water on to their elders' hands and asking for forgiveness for their bad deeds in the past. In return, their elders give them their blessing. People also pour water on to one another to bring about good luck for the New Year. Khaosan Road has become the most popular destination for the water fight among tourists during the Songkran holiday.

Another famous festival is Loy Krathong which celebrates the full moon of the twelfth lunar month. People usually bring their *krathong*, a lotus-shape vessel decorated with banana leaves and flowers, in order to release it into the river. In so doing, they ask for forgiveness for their wrongdoings and express their thanks to the river goddess Phra Mae Khongkha.

A floating krathong is symbolic of bad luck floating away. Loy Krathong will leave all those who take part with unforgettable memories imprinted upon their minds, involving lit candles and the sound of the river illuminated by the full moon. In Bangkok, Chao Phraya River is the main river for celebration.

The influence of kings from the past to the present makes Bangkok different from other global cities, since it is the capital where kings once lived. Their preferences and relationships with foreign countries led to a widespread architectural transformation and the transfer of technical knowledge between foreign and Thai artisans. Another factor which makes Bangkok unique is its urban sprawl; unlike other capital cities, there is no clearly discernible business centre in Bangkok. Rather, it is spread across various districts.

To sum up, the metropolis of Bangkok is simply waiting to welcome visitors of all countries and languages who are eager to explore its art and culture as well as the exquisite architecture on display.

Birthplace of the City

1

020 The Royal Thai Survey Department

021 Grand Vihara, Wat Ratchapradit Sathitmahasimaram Ratchaworawihan

022 The Bhuthorn

023 Dee House

024 Grand Vihara, Wat Ratchabophit Sathitmahasimaram Ratchaworawihan

025 Corrections Museum

026 Salachaloemkrung Royal Theatre

027 National Discovery Museum (Former Office of the Ministry of Commerce)

028 Chakrabongse Palace

029 Long Building, Suan Kulab College

030 Constitutional Court

031 Man Naruemit Building, Debsirin School

032 Varadis Palace (Varadis Palace Museum)

033 Siam Commercial Bank Plc., Chaloem Nakhon Branch

034 Khunying Pornpan Tharanumas Residence

035 Tang Toh Kang Gold Shop

036 Pei Ing School

037 Siam Commercial Bank Plc., Talad Noi Branch

038 Church of the Holy Rosary

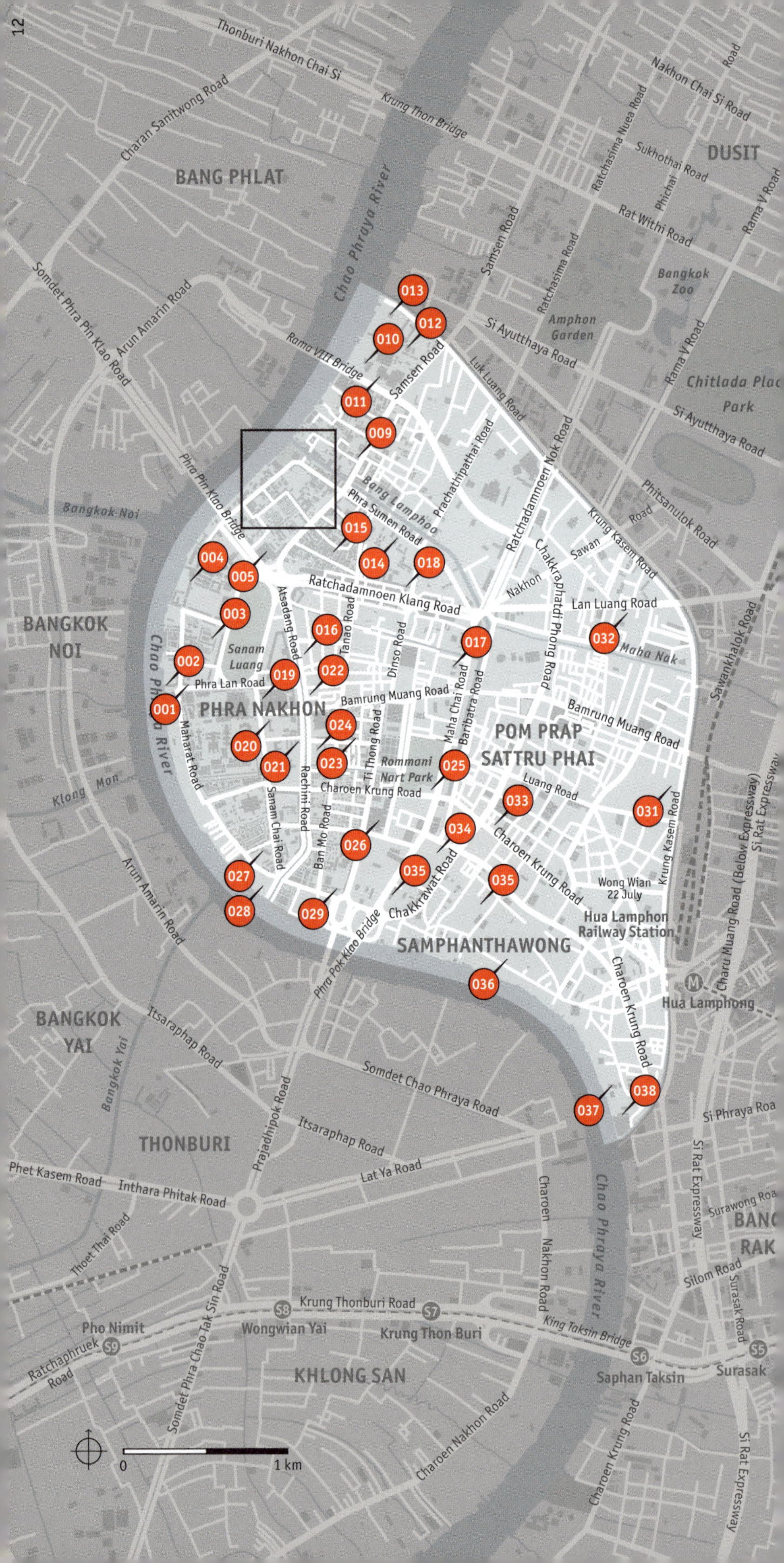
Thonburi Nakhon Chai Si
Krung Thon Bridge
Nakhon Chai Si Road
Road
Charan Sanitwong Road
BANG PHLAT
DUSIT
Ratchasima Nuea Road
Sukhothai Road
Phichai
Rama V Road
Rat Withi Road
Chao Phraya River
Samsen Road
Ratchasima Road
Bangkok Zoo
Amphon Garden
Si Ayutthaya Road
Rama V Road
Chitlada Plac
Park
Si Ayutthaya Road
Somdet Phra Pin Klao Road
Arun Amarin Road
Rama VIII Bridge
Samsen Road
Luk Luang Road
Ratchadamnoen Nok Road
Prachathipathai Road
Bang Lamphoo
Phra Sumen Road
Phitsanulok Road
Road
Phra Pin Klao Bridge
Bangkok Noi
Krung Kasem Road
Sawan
Nakhon
Chakkraphatdi Phong Road
Ratchadamnoen Klang Road
Lan Luang Road
Sawankhalok Road
BANGKOK
NOI
Chao Phraya River
Sanam Luang
Atsadang Road
Tanao Road
Dinso Road
Maha Nak
Phra Lan Road
PHRA NAKHON
Bamrung Muang Road
Maha Chai Road
Baribatra Road
Bamrung Muang Road
POM PRAP
SATTRU PHAI
Maharat Road
Rachini Road
Ti Thong Road
Rommani Nart Park
Charoen Krung Road
Luang Road
Klong Mon
Sanam Chai Road
Ban Mo Road
Charoen Krung Road
Krung Kasem Road
Charu Muang Road (Below Expressway)
Si Rat Expressway
Arun Amarin Road
Chakkrawat Road
Wong Wian 22 July
Hua Lamphon Railway Station
Phra Pok Klao Bridge
SAMPHANTHAWONG
Charoen Krung Road
Hua Lamphong
BANGKOK
YAI
Itsaraphap Road
Bangkok Yai
Somdet Chao Phraya Road
Prajadhipok Road
Si Phraya Road
Itsaraphap Road
THONBURI
Phet Kasem Road
Inthara Phitak Road
Lat Ya Road
Charoen Nakhon Road
Chao Phraya River
Si Rat Expressway
Surawong Road
BANG
RAK
Thoet Thai Road
Silom Road
Surasak Road
Somdet Phra Chao Tak Sin Road
Krung Thonburi Road
S8
S7
Pho Nimit
Wongwian Yai
Krung Thon Buri
King Taksin Bridge
S9
Ratchaphruek Road
S6
S5
KHLONG SAN
Saphan Taksin
Surasak
Charoen Nakhon Road
Charoen Krung Road
Si Rat Expressway
0
1 km
001
002
003
004
005
009
010
011
012
013
014
015
016
017
018
019
020
021
022
023
024
025
026
027
028
029
031
032
033
034
035
035
036
037
038

008
007
006
Phra Sumen Fort
Phra Athit Road
Chakka Phong Road
0
200 m
Sret Siri Road
Thoet Damri Road
Si Rat Expressway
Rama VI Road
Soi Ari Samphan
Ari
N5
Phahon Yothin Road
N4
Sanam Pao
Si Rat
Expressway
Soi Ratchawithi
Ratchawithi Road
Si Rat Expressway
Yothi Road
Victory Monument
N3
Phayathai Road
Rang Nam Road
Ratchaprarop Road
Din Daeng Road
Don Pracha Songkhro
Pracha Songkhro 2
Samsen
Si Ayutthaya Road
Si Ayutthaya Road
N2
Phaya Thai
Chaloem Maha
Nakhon Expressway
Si Rat Expressway
Phet Buri Road
RATCHATHEWI
Ratchaprarop
Asok Din Daeng Road
N1
Phet Buri Road
Ratchathewi
Road
Phet Buri Road
Phetchaburi
Saen Saep
Rama I Road
W1
National
Stadium
CEN
Siam
Ratchadamri
Chit Lom
E1
Phloen Chit Road
Witthayu Road
E2
Phloen Chit
Soi Sukhumvit 3
Soi Sukhumvit 13
Soi Sukhumvit 21
PATHUM WAN
Phayathai Road
Road
Soi Lang Suan
Soi Ruam Ruedi
Chaloem Maha Nakhon Expressway
E3
Nana
Soi Sukhumvit 4
Sukhumvit
Road
E4
Asok
S1
Ratchadamri
Henri Dunant Road
Ratchadamri
Sarasin Road
Suan
Lumphini
Lake
Sam Yan
Lumphini
Park
Si Lom
Witthayu Road
Soi Plukchit
Lake
Ratchada
Soi Sukhumvit 16
Ratchadaphisek Road
S2
Sala Daeng
Rama IV Road
Lumphini
Queen Sirikit
National
Conv. Centre
S3
Sathon Tai Road
Khong Toei
Rama IV Road
Soi Suan Phlu
Naradhiwas Rajanagarindra Road
Yen Akat Road
Chaloem Maha Nakhon Expressway
Sunthon Kosa Road
SATHON
Nang Lychee Road
Rama III Road

Silpakorn University Art Gallery 001 A

Location Wang Tha Phra Campus, Na Phra Lan Road
Architect Joachim Grassi (Phra Tamnak Klang/Middle Pavilion)
Owner/proprietor Silpakorn University
Construction period King Rama I period (Thong Phra Rong), King Rama V period (Phra Tamnak Klang)
Conservation award 1989

Silpakorn University Art Gallery was part of the Wang Tha Phra compound, built in the reign of King Rama I as the residence of Chaofa Krommakhun Kasttranuchit. Later, during the reign of King Rama II, it became the official residence of Krommamuen Jessadabodin (King Rama III). Ever since the prince ascended to the throne in 1824, it has been resided in by several other princes. During the reign of King Rama V, the palace was the official residence of Prince Krommamuen Adulyalaksanasombat. The last resident was Prince Krommaphraya Narissaranuwattiwong. During this period, the Phra Tamnak Klang (Middle Pavilion) was designed in a neo-classical style to connect to Phra Tamnak Phannarai, a residence of the Prince's mother. Nowadays, Thong Phra Klang has been rehabilitated to house the university art gallery, where numerous art exhibitions and events are held throughout the year.

≈ Thanachart Bank Plc., Tha Phra Chan Branch 002 A

Location 196–198 Maharat Road
Architect/designer Unknown
Owner/proprietor Thanachart Bank Plc.
Construction period King Rama V period
Conservation award 1994

The Tha Phra Chan branch of Siam City Bank Plc. is situated in an ancient shophouse in the Tha Chang Wang Luang area. The building was created during the period of King Rama V in a neo-classical style. The front façade comprises three porches decorated with fractables – a typical feature of Dutch architecture. The walls are rusticated with round arched windows visible on the upper storey and segmental arched ones on the ground floor. The Siam City Bank Plc. has rented the building from the Crown Property Bureau since 1969. It commissioned the repair and renovation of the building to suit the bank's function as well as to restore its original features.

≚ Thawon Watthu Building 003 A

Location Na Phra That Road
Architect HRH Prince Krommaphraya Narisaranuwattiwong
Owner/proprietor The Fine Arts Department
Construction period 1895–1916
Conservation award 2007

Thawon Watthu Building is a brick masonry building with influences of Khmer architecture. The aesthetically pleasing design is similar to that of Angkor Wat. The building comprises three four-sided porticos and a curved tiled roof. During the reign of King Rama VII, Thawon Watthu Building housed King Rama VI's books and newspapers. It was then renamed *Ho Phra Samut Vajiravudh*. Later, the Fine Arts Department renovated some parts of the building to use as the Narathip Centre for Social Science Research (in commemoration of Prince Krommamuen Narathipphongpraphan) as well as the headquarters for its architectural faculty of global renown.

Dome Building, Thammasat University 004 A

Location Thammasat University, Phra Chan Road
Architect Mue Abhaiwongse
Owner/proprietor Thammasat University
Construction period 1935–1936
Conservation award 2005

Dome Building, the administration hall, involved the renovation of four buildings featuring two storeys which were built in the reign of King Rama VI. These were realised with a Western-style architecture and are laid out in a neat row facing the river. Later, the roof was built to connect the buildings. A three-storey building has been developed in the open areas between the second and third buildings with a dome to form a symbolic landmark. In the period from 1960 to 1977, the university ordered the fourth building on the Tha Phra Athit wing to be demolished to build the AT Room. The first building was demolished to build a multi-purpose hall. Later, in 1984, the university constructed the Pridi Phanomyong Monument and renovated the Dome Building the following year by extending a portico to the rear which serves as Pridi Phanomyong Memorial Hall. The building is designed in modern reinforced concrete with plastered brick walls featuring brown tiles. At present, the Dome Building houses the Thammasat University Historical Hall of Fame, a centre for the exhibition and dissemination of the history of the university and its former students in their various professions.

The National Gallery (The Royal Mint) 005 A

Location 4 Chaofa Road, Phra Borommaharatchawang
Architect Carlo Allegri
Proprietor The Fine Arts Department
Construction period 1902
Conservation award 1989

The National Gallery was originally the Royal Mint named Roang Krasap Sitthikan. It was built around the year 1902 during the reign of King Rama V and was designed by the Italian engineer Carlo Allegri in a neo-Palladian style. The entrance porch is decorated with the national emblem of Thailand on the pediment. The rectangular plan surrounds an open courtyard where a water tank with steel stands is located. At the time, the Mint used very advanced technology imported from Europe to manufacture coins with value of up to 80,000 to 100,000 baht per day. It was officially opened in 1902 and operated prior to its relocation in 1968. In 1974, the property was transformed into an art gallery.

≈ Nine-Room Terraced Building on Phra Arthit Road 006 A

Location 82–98 Phra Arthit Road
Architect Unknown
Owner/proprietor The Bureau of the Crown Property
Construction period 1947
Conservation award 2008

A nine-room terraced building located on Phra Arthit Road (Soi Chanasongkarm) is regarded by many to be one of the most fantastic antique buildings in Bangkok, since it prominently stands out from the other buildings on the road. It consists of two floors and nine rooms with a rectangular tiled roof, *Kra Beuang Waow*. Each room has a veranda built on to the front of the building. The Bureau of the Crown Property, which is renting out the buildings on this street to private investors, recently renovated the building and took pains to restore its original structure. Since the buildings on this road are now more than fifty years old, they have regrettably become dilapidated with the passage of time. In light of the fact that they were originally too small, tenants have thus expanded them to accommodate their businesses and living quarters. This, however, has exerted a negative impact on the structure itself. The restoration project by the Bureau of the Crown Property is considered a prototype of a conservative project. The project began in 2003 and was completed in 2007.

Phra Athit Residence 007 A

Location 102/1 Phra Athit Road
Architect Unknown
Owner/proprietor The Manager Plc.
Construction period 1926–1927
Conservation award 1999

The two-storey Phra Athit Residence is an example of Arts and Crafts architecture. On the right wing is a three-storey tower with a pyramid dome which is decorated with stucco and intricate wood carvings. Its overall appearance is rather simple, in keeping with the modern architecture which dominated Thailand in the reign of King Rama VII. The house was originally the palace of Prince Pongseisares who was the minister of the royal household under King Rama II. After the prince passed away, the house was inherited by Chaophraya Woraphongphipat, the minister of the royal household under King Rama V. He in turn replaced the old palace with a new house called *Baan Phra Athit*. After Chaophraya Woraphongphipat then passed away, the house was rented to the German Institution of Culture (Goethe) from the period between 1962 and 1987. It was then sold to The Manager Plc. Several new buildings were added to the compound which has been conserved and is used as an office.

« Rows of Housing on Phra Athit Road 008 A

Location Phra Athit Road, Chanasongkhram
Proprietor The Crown Property Bureau
Construction period ca. King Rama VI period
Conservation award 2001

The rows of housing on Phra Athit Road are similar to those on Thanow Road: two-storey brick and mortar buildings with a wall-bearing system. These have mostly been renovated as restaurants and pubs, although there are a few businesses too. The façades have been modified to resemble commercial-like buildings and are far more colourful than the originals. The roofing material, meanwhile, consists of diamond-shaped cement tiles. The buildings have a folding wooden door that can be fully opened for commercial purposes. All buildings have been well conserved. Tenants have predominantly preferred to decorate the buildings in antique styles which are in harmony with original architectural features. Therefore, these rows of housing still retain their value as historic buildings as well as being functional and operating efficiently in terms of today's standards.

« Phra Nakorn District Office 009 A

Location 78 Samsen Road, Wat Sam Phraya
Architect Unknown
Owner/proprietor Phra Nakorn District
Construction period 1914
Conservation award 2002

Phraya Amaretsombat Residence is a brick masonry building in keeping with the Arts and Crafts movement. It has a hipped gable roof and two porches on the western side and was built by a contractor from Hong Kong. The interior is finely decorated with patterned teak parquets, mouldings, stucco and collared glass panes. The original plan of the house was U-shaped with an open fountain court in the middle, but the court was later roofed to be used as a foyer. It originally belonged to Phraya Amaretsombat, head of the revenue department in the reign of King Rama VI. After the Second World War, he sold this house to Chawi Komolkiti. It was later sold again and used as the Vietnamese Embassy from 1953 to 1973, before being acquired by the Bangkok Metropolitan. Today it is used as the Phra Nakhon district office.

1

Bang Khun Phrom Palace, Tamnak Yai and Tamnak Somdej 010 A

Location Bank of Thailand, Bang Khunphrom Junction
Architects Mario Tamagno (Tamnak Yai – Main Pavilion); Karl Duhring (Tamnak Somdej)
Owner/proprietor Bank of Thailand
Construction period 1901
Conservation award 1993

The Tamnak Yai mansion of Bang Khun Phrom Palace is a two-storey building built in a neo-baroque style. The middle porch comprises pillars and an arch, above which are windows denoting Palladian motifs and a distinguished pair of twisted columns elaborately decorated with stucco. The left wing is a three-storey tower, whereas the right wing has two storeys and a curvilinear plan. Tamnak Yai has been rehabilitated to house the Bank of Thailand Museum. As for Tamnak Somdej, it boasts a Jugendstil, or German Art Nouveau, architecture. The interior is decorated with mural paintings created by Carlo Rigoli, an Italian artist. It was built in 1913 as a residence for Queen Sukhumalmarasi. Between 1902 and 1932, the palace was a centre of various fields of arts. It was also a school for princesses and young ladies from noble families, who were taught by foreign teachers, and adopted the name Bang Khun Phrom University.

« Bank of Thailand 011 A

Location Bang Khunphrom Junction
Architects Plan Architects Co., Ltd.
Owner/proprietor Bank of Thailand
Construction period Unknown
Architectural design award 2009

The concept behind the design for the Bank of Thailand was to use space efficiently and create a healthy environment with energy-efficient appliances and the use of natural light. The overall design is simple but, at the same time, modern and elegant which suits the high-level State official building. The layout of the building and its open spaces perfectly fits within

the compound. Despite its efficient use of energy and the healthy outdoor environment which is abundant with lush greenery, the building has not yet met several standards in relation to green architecture. It is nevertheless considered a good starting point for energy efficiency in terms of government buildings.

≈ Building No. 4, Bank of Thailand 012 A

Location Bank of Thailand, Samsen Road
Architect Emilio Gollo
Owner/proprietor Bank of Thailand
Construction period 1917–1918
Conservation award 2004

The palace was built under the orders of King Rama VI as a residence for Prince Krommaphraya Thewawongwaropaka, the first Minister of Foreign Affairs. Tuek Mom Lamai is a brick masonry structure built in a neo-Palladian style with five bays. The building spans three storeys in height which is signified by three dormers projecting from the roof. The ground floor mostly comprises solid walls, while the second floor is surrounded by verandas with double Ionic columns and balustrades gleaming in resplendent white. The third floor, meanwhile, has doors that open on to balconies which are surrounded by balustrades.

Cooperative Auditing Department 013 A

Location Bank of Thailand, Samsen Road
Architects Emilio Gollo
Owner/proprietor Bank of Thailand
Construction period 1917 – 1918
Conservation award 2004

The Department of Cooperative Auditing was founded in the year 1917. The tasteful building originally formed part of the Wang Thewet palace compound, the residence of Prince Krommaphra Chanthaburinaruenat. Later, Mom Chao Khachonchob Kittikhun sold the property to the Ministry of Agri-

culture and Cooperatives in the year 1965. The building has a total of three storeys and is an impressive example of art nouveau architecture which is modestly decorated. A spacious attic has been built beneath the hipped gable roof. The building boasts a clean white façade, lending it a minimalist appearance. Its historic significance lies in the fact that Her Majesty Queen Sirikit used to reside here during her childhood. At present, it houses the minister's office, a library rich in resources, and an information centre of the Department of Cooperative Auditing.

ตำหนักเพ็ชร

« Tamnak Phet, Wat Bowonniwetwihan 014 A

Location Wat Bowonniwetwihan, Phra Sumen Road, Bowonniwet
Architect Unknown
Owner/proprietor Wat Bowonniwetwihan
Construction period 1913
Conservation award 1996

Wat Bowonniwetwihan was originally a local temple with the name Wat Mai, or Wat Bon. Somdet Phra Boworaratchao Mahasakdipholasep, the Vice-King of King Rama II, reestablished it as a royal temple between 1824 and 1832. King Rama III renamed the temple Wat Bowonniwetwihan in 1836. At that time, the abbot was King Rama IV, his brother, when he was ordained as a monk. The temple has been developed and maintained in every successive reign. Therefore, it comprises several valuable architectural and art objects, one of which is Tamnak Phet, a throne hall combining Western and Thai influences. King Rama VI had the building constructed in 1913 to be used as a single-storey throne hall for Somdet Phra Maha Samanachao Krommaphra Wachirayan Warorot, the Supreme Patriarch. It has a hipped roof and gabled entrance porch with colonnades at the front and is decorated with elaborate woodcarvings.

¥ Khao San Museum 015 A

Location Khao San Road
Architect Chao Phraya Athonthurasin
Owner/proprietor Sansern Kraichitti
Construction period ca. 1909
Conservation award 2005

Kraichitti Residence was created out of love since Chao Phraya Athonthurasin built it as a wedding present for his daughter. It is a two-storey building with a hipped roof and a gable at the front porch, decorated with wood openwork. The architecture is in a colonial style with verandas enclosed by cement balustrades and classic French windows, whose upper parts are wooden louvres and lower parts wooden panels. The wooden-framed headlights are infilled with translucent glass panels. The exterior is decorated with simple moulding. By contrast, the interior is a blend of several styles in an eclectic manner. At present, Kraichitti Residence is rented out to Chez Bruno Restaurant. The upper floor of the house is divided into three separate rooms. The first room houses an exhibition on the history of Rattanakosin Island and the second of the Kraichitti family, while the last room has been furbished as an art gallery.

« Issarasena House 016 A

Location Asadang Road
Owner/proprietor Lieutenant Nurak and Phiphatphong Issarasena Na Ayutthaya
Construction period King Rama V period
Conservation award 2004

Issarasena House has a long history dating back to 1887, when the house belonged to Prince Thongthaemthawalyawong, the thirty-ninth son of King Rama IV. It used to serve as a residence for foreign medical doctors. The principal building is a two-storey brick wall-bearing structure built in a colonial style. Judging from this, the date of construction is estimated to fall in the reign of King Rama V. The building has a hipped roof decorated with stucco mouldings. The house is quite simple in decoration but has well-balanced and dignified proportions. Phiphatphong Issarasena Na Ayutthaya initiated the conservation of the house which took as long as fifteen years. It will be handed down to future generations as a valuable asset.

⬎ Wannasilpsamoson, Wat Thepthidaram 017 A

Location Sangkhawas Zone, Wat Thepthidaram, Mahachai Road, Samramrat
Architect Unknown
Owner/proprietor Wat Thepthidaram
Construction period 1836–1839
Conservation award 1994

Sunthorn Phu or Phra Sunthornwoharn, the great poet of Rattnakosin, was ordained as a monk for fifteen years and spent three years in Wat Thepthidaram. His *kuti* (residence) was part of the Sangkhawas zone (residential area for monks). The building is a U-shaped brick structure with a courtyard in the middle. The design is a blend of Thai and Chinese architecture with a Western-style gateway. The building comprises four to five rooms; the room on the left of the northern gateway is the former residence of Sunthorn Phu. It is thought that he composed many of his principal works during his stay at Wat Thepthidaram, which has currently been conserved in Sunthorn Phu's honour. The place has now been given the title Wannasilpsamoson (Literature Club) and his works are presented here.

≽ McDonald's, Ratchadamnoen Branch 018 A

Location 77/1 Ratchadamnoen Klang Road, Bowonniwet
Architect Mom Luang Pum Malakul
Owner McThai Co., Ltd.
Construction period 1943
Conservation award 2001

The Ratchadamnoen branch of McDonald's is one of the buildings located in the four corners of the Democracy Monument. The single-storey buildings are built in reinforced concrete and designed in a distinct modernist style. The curved plan of the building conforms to the shape of the roundabout. It has an open front and semicircular porch at each end. Originally, buildings in this location were used to observe marching troops. When such ceremonies were later relocated, the buildings were rented to private investors for commercial use. McThai Co. Ltd., the fourth tenant, aimed to rehabilitate the building by adopting a conservative approach and thus contacted the Fine Arts Department to be their project advisor, which led to the successful integration of new elements and colours.

≈ Ministry of Defence 019 A

Location Sanamchai Road
Architect Joachim Grassi
Owner/proprietor Ministry of Defence
Construction period 1882–1884
Conservation award 1997

The building is distinguished by its neo-classical architecture which is realised in a neo-Palladian style. This is expressed by a virtually square plan surrounding an inner court and a front porch facing west. The façades are decorated with the gilded emblem of the Royal Guard on the pediment, a superimposed order of pilasters and the emblem of the Ministry of Defence on the balcony parapet, which was a later addition. In times of yore, the area was home to three palaces which were demolished at a later stage and replaced by other buildings, such as a stable for horses and a silk factory. King Rama V commissioned a barracks hall to be built here during his reign as a place where soldiers, weapons, vehicles and provisions were all stationed. Originally named the Front Barracks, the title was later changed to Ministry of Defence.

» The Royal Thai Survey Department 020 A

Location Kalayanamaitri Road, Phra Borommaharatchawang, Phra Nakhon
Architect Stefano Cardu
Owner Supreme Command Headquarters
Construction period ca. 1891
Conservation award 1984

Survey works systematically began in Thailand during King Rama V's reign under the recommendation of Henry Alabaster. Consequently, the first Survey School was founded in 1883, while 3 September 1885 saw the establishment of the Survey Department with Phra Wiphakphuwadon (James McCarthy) as director. As for the building, it was built around 1891 as part of Saranrom Palace and was formerly a military school. It then became the Chief of Staff Department before being appointed the headquarters of the Royal Thai Survey Department in 1931. Later, after having been united with the Royal Thai Army Survey Department in 1963, the organisation was renamed the Royal Thai Survey Department. The building is in a neo-classical style which is accentuated by the massive porches – particularly the one in the middle – decorated with a fractable on which the emblem of King Rama V and Erawan, the legendary three-headed elephant, are embellished.

Grand Vihara, Wat Ratchapradit Sathitmaha-simaram Ratchaworawihan 021 A

Location 2 Rachini Road, Borommaharatchawang
Architect Phraya Ratchasongkhram
Owner/proprietor Wat Ratchapradit Sathitmahasimaram Ratchaworawihan
Construction period 1864
Conservation award 1989

The temple built in the fourth reign of Rattanakosin, entitled Wat Ratchapradit Athitmahasimaram Ratchaworawihan, was founded in 1864 by King Rama IV. There are several important architectural and art objects in the compound, with the Grand Vihara and a bell-shaped pagoda constituting the most eye-catching structures. The Royal Seal of King Rama IV is depicted with gilded lacquer on the pediment. The rear wall of the building is installed with inscriptions providing information on the date of establishment and the circumscription of the temple's sacred boundary (*sema*). It is worthy to note that the sacred boundary of this temple circumscribes the temple's walls, enabling the Grand Vihara to function as an ordination hall since it is also included within the sacred area. An image of a Buddha – Phra Phuttha Sihingkhapatimakon, a replica of Phra Phutthasihing – is enshrined in the hall. The interior is decorated with a number of mural paintings, including one depicting the King's legendary trip to Tambon Wa Ko in order to observe the eclipse of the sun in the year 1868.

≈ The Bhuthorn 022 A

Location 96–98 Phraeng Bhuthorn Road, Phra Nakhon
Architects Direk and Chitlada Senglaung (renovation)
Owner/proprietor Direk and Chitlada Senglaung
Construction period King Rama V period
Conservation award 2010

The Bhuthorn is one of the terraced houses rented by Prince Bhutharesdhamrongsak, Prince Narathipprapanphong and Prince Salpasartsupphakit to gain revenue for residents. The building is part of a row of two-storey housing with narrow façades, diamond-shaped roof tiles, masonry wall bearings, polished wooden floors, metal balusters in the windows and a series of folding wooden doors. The current owner has tried to preserve the original character of the building by maintaining the old structure and decorating it with replicas of the old – i.e. floors with handmade tiles featuring floral motifs, gingerbread-style eaves, antique furniture with a touch of Thai fabric and rattan accents. This helps create a colonial atmosphere while maintaining guests' utmost comfort. Currently, the Bhuthorn has been registered as a conserved building under the Crown Property Bureau, while Phraeng Bhuthorn Road is registered as a well-conserved community to the Fine Arts Department.

≫ Dee House 023 A

Location 123 Fueang Nakhon Road, Sathitmahasimaram
Owner/proprietor Songsith Charuparn
Construction period King Rama V period
Conservation award 1996

Baan Dee is a shophouse with discernibly Western-influenced architecture, similar to the shophouses in Singapore to arise towards the end of King Rama V's reign. It comprises a brick masonry wall-bearing structure. The ground floor is open for commercial purposes while the second floor is a dwelling. The house is roofed with cement tiles decorated with stucco and fretwork. It was originally the residence of Captain Luang Bamrungyuth, who was given it by King Rama V. Later, he let it to a small publishing house until circa 1990. His heir ordered its repair with the strict instructions to preserve all original features. Today it is used as a coffee shop.

Grand Vihara, Wat Ratchabophit Sathitmaha-simaram Ratchaworawihan 024 A

Location Ratchabophit Road, Wat Ratchabophit
Architect Unknown
Owner/proprietor Wat Ratchabophit Sathitmahasimaram Ratchaworawihan
Construction period 1869–1870
Conservation award 2007

Wat Ratchabophit Sathitmahasimaram Ratchaworawihan is a royal temple of the first rank. Following the ancient royal tradition, the temple was established by King Rama V between 1869 and 1870. However, it was the last to be founded by order of the King based on this tradition. The special feature of the Maha Sima temple is that monks' religious activities are not only confined to the *ubosatha* (ordination hall), but can be performed anywhere within its boundaries. The walls are built of plastered brick and are decorated with glazed tiles, while the window panels are decorated with gilded black lacquer on the inside. The golden *chedi* (pagoda) is surmounted by a resplendent golden ball which was built in a Sri Lankan style.

iStock/Warayoo

≈ Corrections Museum 025 A

Location 436 Mahachai Road, Samranrat, Phra Nakhon
Architect Joachim Grassi
Owner/proprietor Thai Department of Corrections, Ministry of Interior
Construction period 1889
Conservation award 1997

The Corrections Museum, a former prison, is an example of neo-renaissance architecture. The history of the Department of Corrections and information on various forms of punishment meted out since ancient times are presented here, while a building called Cell Block 9 has been preserved. The prison was built under the orders of King Rama V. It was planned to follow the Brixton Prison of England, according to Phraya Chaiwichitsitthisastra, a senior official who had worked at the Royal Thai Embassy in London. The prison operated for more than 103 years until 1991, when prisoners were moved to a new prison and the cabinet passed a resolution to convert the area into a public park and the building into a museum. The project was intended to commemorate the Queen's sixtieth birthday anniversary. On 7 August 1999, the Crown Prince presided over the opening ceremony of the museum and the park, which the King named Suan Rommaninath.

Salachaloemkrung Royal Theatre 026 A

Location 66 Charoen Krung Road
Architect Mom Chao Samaichaloem Kridakon
Owner Chaloem Krung Manitas Co., Ltd.
Construction period 1930–1933
Conservation award 1994

Salachaloemkrung Royal Theatre boasts an impressive history since it was built to commemorate Bangkok's 150th anniversary celebrations in 1936. King Rama VII therefore named the theatre *Sala Chloem Krung*, meaning City Celebration Pavilion. Construction commenced on 1 July 1930, with King Rama VII presiding over the placing of the foundation stone. The architecture is in the style of Bauhaus. The theatre is simple and clearly interpretable by its pure form. For the opening ceremony on 2 July 1933, a sound-on-film motion picture was shown for the first time in Thailand.

» National Discovery Museum (Former Office of the Ministry of Commerce) 027 A

Location Sanamchai Road
Architect Mario Tamagno
Owner/proprietor National Discovery Museum Institute
Construction period ca. 1921–1922
Conservation award 2006

The Ministry of Commerce, formerly called the Department of Commerce and Statistical Forecasts, was elevated to a ministry by King Rama VI on 20 August 1920. The Office of the Ministry of Commerce was constructed on land formerly belonging to the princes, sons of King Rama III. This building, intentionally designed as an office building, is one of the first of its kind in Thailand. Construction began circa 1921 and was completed in 1922. The architectural style is classic revival, with the distinctive use of colossal order. In 1989, the Ministry of Commerce moved to a new office at Nonthaburi. The former office building was left deserted until the National Discovery Museum Institute (NDMI) was established in the year 2004, an institute which recognised the significance of the building in terms of history, architecture and setting. Therefore, the NDMI commissioned its conservation and restoration which commenced in 2005, seeking to preserve all original features.

» Chakrabongse Palace 028 A

Location Maharat Road
Architect Ercole Manfredi, Edward Healey (extension)
Owner/proprietor Mom Ratchawong Narisa Chakrabongse
Construction period 1909–1910
Conservation award 1987

Chakrabongse Palace was originally called Wang Tha Tian (Tha Tian Palace). The riverside pavilion amidst tranquil settings was home to Prince Chakrabongsebhuvanat and Lady Kathrin, his wife. It was also intended to be a domicile for their son, Prince Chulachakrabongse. The architecture is in a domestic revival style with two storeys at the front, three storeys on the left wing and a tower housing the relics of King Rama V and Queen Si Patcharinthra. There is a porch at the front and terrace at the rear. The house currently belongs to Mom Ratchawong Narisa Chakrabongse, the daughter of Prince Chulachakrabongse, who takes care of the house, foundations and offices of the family, which are situated in an outbuilding by Maharat Road.

» Long Building, Suan Kulab College 029 A

Location 88 Tri Pet Road, Wangburapha Phirom
Architect Unknown
Owner/proprietor Suan Kulab College
Construction period 1910
Conservation award 2000

Tuek Yao (Long Building) is built in a neoclassical style and was completed in the reign of King V. It has two storeys, while the walls are fitted with arched windows on the side overlooking the road and arcades on the inner side. The entrance, a Palladian motif, is an arched gateway underneath a gable roof, flanked by rectangular gateways on both sides. The building was initially built by Wat Ratchaburana on request of the Ministry of Education, who promised to rent the building from the temple when it was finished. During the Second World War, the building was partially destroyed by bombs and had to be reconstructed to its original features.

» Constitutional Court 030 A

Location Chakpet Road, Wang Buraphaphirom
Architect Unknown
Owner/proprietor Constitutional Court
Construction period King Rama V period
Conservation award 2001

The Constitutional Court was originally a residence of Chao Phraya Rattanathibet

(Phum Sichaiyant), who was Prime Minister during the reign of King Rama V. The three-storey house is an example of a simple renaissance revival architecture. The lowest storey features rusticated walls and arched windows similar to those of Italian palazzos. The upper two storeys have rectangular windows in a repeated rhythm which are decorated with mouldings displaying simple designs. The existing building comprises the original house to the south, while the northern part was added at a later stage. The Ministry of Interior bought the house in 1902 to serve as a reception house for State guests. Later, in 1908, King Rama V ordered the Ministry of Education to move into this house. An extension to the northern part was thus carried out between the years 1920 and 1922. Later, it became an office for government organisations until the Constitutional Court was established. The Fine Arts Department was assigned to restore the building, a process which was eventually completed in 2001.

แม้นศึกษาสถาน

« Man Naruemit Building, Debsirin School 031 A

Architect HRH Prince Krommaphraya Narisaranuwattiwong (design), Phian Sombatpiam (reconstruction)
Owner/proprietor Debsirin School
Construction period ca. 1901–1902
Reconstruction 1948–1949
Conservation award 2007

King Rama V aimed to promote education to the public. Therefore, he ordered His Royal Highness Prince Krommaphraya Damrongrachanubhap to establish Debsirin School on 15 March 1885 to serve the general public. In the early days, the school used the Sala Kan Parian (Gathering Hall) of Wat Debsirintharawat as its study hall. The two-storey Maen Naruemit Building is an example of a gothic revival architecture whose prominent features include pointed arched doors and windows, stucco and pilasters which accentuate the vertical lines and the building's height. The façade boasts a resplendent shade of red, lending it a striking appearance.

≽ Varadis Palace (Varadis Palace Museum) 032 A

Location 204 Lan Luang Road
Architect Karl Duhring
Owner/proprietor Major General Mom Ratchawong Sangkadis Diskul
Construction period 1910–1911
Conservation award 1984

Wang Varadis (Varadis Palace) was originally a residence of Prince Krommaphraya Damrong Rajanubhab, who was regarded as the father of Thai history during the Ratanakosin period. The palace was built from 1910 to 1911 on land which belonged to his mother, Chaochom Manda Chum, a consort of King Rama IV. The construction was funded by King Rama VI. The style of architecture of the two-storey palace is Jugendstil, or German Art Nouveau. It has a high-pitched hipped gable roof tiled with local terracotta roof tiles sourced from Songkhla. Its appearance is sturdy and resolute, yet dynamic and gentle at the same time.

» Siam Commercial Bank Plc., Chaloem Nakhon Branch 033 A

Location 269 Charoen Krung-Worachak Roads, Pom Prap, Pom Prapsattruphai
Architect/designer Unknown
Owner The Crown Property Bureau
Construction period King Rama V period
Conservation award 2007

The Chaloem Nakhon branch of Siam Commercial Bank Plc. is situated within an old building that was originally a leading department store during the late King Rama V period. It went by the name S.E.C. Store. The headquarters of Siam Commercial Bank Plc. consist of a reinforced concrete structure featuring three storeys at the corner and two storeys on the wings, covered by a hipped roof. Owing to the fact that the building is located at a junction, this means that its corner is designed in a beautiful sweeping curved form. The architecture is markedly neoclassical in style. Siam Commercial Bank Plc. rented the building from the Crown Property Bureau to be used as their headquarters. The bank has redecorated and conserved this building with special attention given towards its historic value, which is in line with the bank's policy as far as conversions are concerned.

» Khunying Pornpan Tharanumas Residence 034 A

Location 135–137–139 Trok Ya Chun, Samphanthawong
Owner Khunying Pornpan Tharanumas
Construction period King Rama III to the early King Rama IV period
Conservation award 1984

The residential dwelling named Khunying Pornpan Tharanumas (Watcharaphai) consists of three houses: two of them built with clear Chinese architectural influences between the late King Rama III period and the early King Rama IV period, the other in a European style. The latter was built in the King Rama V period to replace the former Chinese building on site. The dwelling originally served as a gambling house called Rong Bon Saphan Hua. Thongkham Tang exchanged a plot of land for the gambling house and renovated it to form his own residence. The property has been inherited by his heirs right up to the present owner, his great granddaughter. The houses are built in a U-shape with an open court at the front. The middle house is a European-inspired building featuring distinctive arched windows, although these have been roofed over with Chinese terracotta roof tiles.

» Tang Toh Kang Gold Shop 035 A

Location 35 Soi Vanit 1,
Mangkon Road, Samphanthawong
Architect/designer Unknown
Proprietor The Crown Property Bureau
Construction period 1921
Conservation award 2000

Tang Toh Kang Gold Shop is the oldest goldsmith in the Sampeng district. It is a seven-storey building with late classical influences, built during the reign of King Rama VI. The building is decorated with stucco and stained glass window panels. In 2000, Her Royal Highness Princess Maha Chakri Sirindhorn paid a visit to Yaowarat Road and Tang Toh Kang Gold Shop. Later, the Tantikan family commissioned a major restoration under supervision of the Fine Arts Department. The restoration was completed in early 2002. Today, the shop has opened some parts of the building as a museum to exhibit the history of the shop and to provide visitors with information on gold crafting.

โรงเรียนเผยอิง
培英學校

« Pei Ing School 036 A

Location 831 Song Wad Road, Chakrawad, Samphanthawong
Architect/designer Unknown
Proprietor The Teo Chiw Society of Thailand and Pei Ing School Committee
Construction period 1916
Conservation award 2002

Pei Ing is a Chinese school whose long history stretches back to the King Rama VI period. The school was founded by Phra Anuwatratchaniyom (Tae Ti Young), Ko Hui Jia, Kow Pid Ji, Siao Kiang Ling, Tang Ho Sang and other Chinese merchants. The school building was built in 1916; four years later construction was completed. The school was officially opened on 24 May 1920 and has been in business for more than eighty years. The architecture is colonial in style with neoclassical influences. Its rectangular plan surrounds an open court in the middle enclosed by rusticated walls, while the entrance is accentuated by a gable porch where a clock is installed on the pediment, decorated with stucco. The façade is in a pastel shade of daffodil yellow.

¥ Siam Commercial Bank Plc., Talad Noi Branch 037 A

Location Talad Noi, Samphanthawong
Architect Annibale Rigotti
Proprietor Siam Commercial Bank Plc.
Date of construction 1908
Conservation award 1982

The Talad Noi branch of the Siam Commercial Bank Plc. is the first bank across Thailand to have been established under the initiation of Prince Krommamuen Mahisararatchaharuethai, the father of Thai Banking, who firstly set up an experimental bank called Book Club after visiting Europe in 1897. The business went well – King Rama V thus granted a royal charter to officially designate the Book Club as the Siam Commercial Bank on 30 January 1906. The three-storey building is an example of beaux arts architecture, expressed by the detailed articulation of the façades. In spite of considerable advances in its fortunes, the bank has always been more than proud to preserve the original value and authenticity of the historic place in which it finds itself.

Church of the Holy Rosary 038 A

Location Talad Noi, Samphanthawong
Architect/designer Father Desalles
Proprietor Wat Mae Phra Lukprakham (Galvar) Church
Construction period 1891–1897
Conservation award 1987

The Church of the Holy Rosary (Galvar) is an ancient Portuguese Catholic church founded by a group of Portuguese priests. In 1786, King Rama I granted them permission to build it. In the same year, the first church was thus built and named Galvario, which was later shortened to Galvar, as it is known today. Facing the river, it was built between the years 1891 and 1897. It has a cross-shaped plan, while its architecture is gothic revival in style. The front façade comprises a pitched-roof bell tower with a cross at the top, a pointed arched gate and a high-pitched gothic gable. The walls are decorated with stained glass depicting scenes from the Bible. The church celebrated its centenary on 5 October 1997.

West Banks of the River

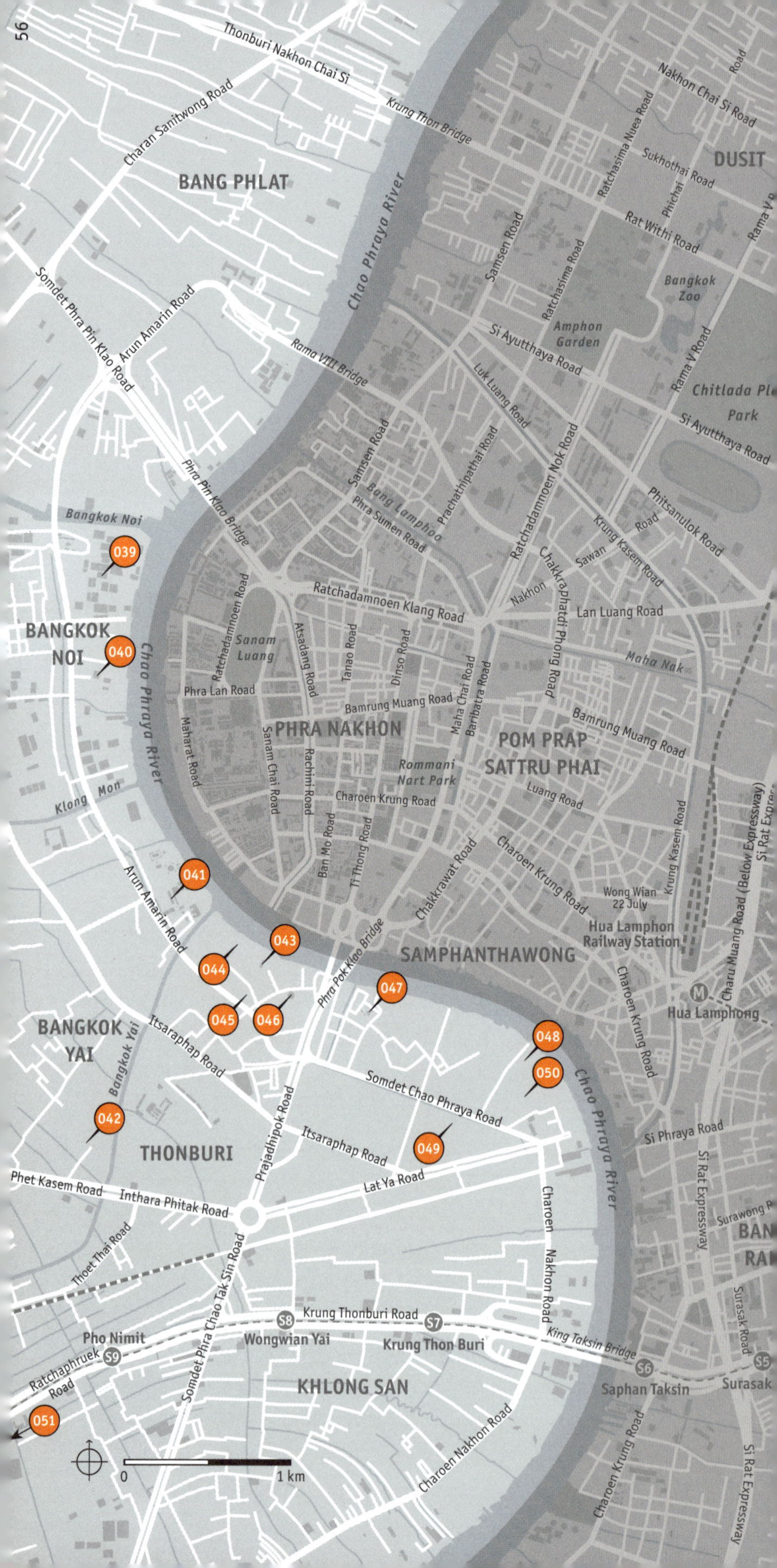
Thonburi Nakhon Chai Si
Krung Thon Bridge
Nakhon Chai Si Road
Road
DUSIT
Charan Sanitwong Road
BANG PHLAT
Ratchasima Nuea Road
Sukhothai Road
Phichai
Rat Withi Road
Rama V
Chao Phraya River
Samsen Road
Ratchasima Road
Bangkok Zoo
Somdet Phra Pin Klao Road
Arun Amarin Road
Rama VIII Bridge
Amphon Garden
Si Ayutthaya Road
Rama V Road
Chitlada Pl
Park
Luk Luang Road
Si Ayutthaya Road
Samsen Road
Prachathipathai Road
Ratchadamnoen Nok Road
Phra Pin Klao Bridge
Bang Lamphoo
Phra Sumen Road
Phitsanulok Road
Krung Kasem Road
Road
Bangkok Noi
Sawan
Chakkraphatdi Phong Road
Nakhon
039
Ratchadamnoen Klang Road
Lan Luang Road
BANGKOK NOI
040
Ratchadamnoen Road
Sanam Luang
Atsadang Road
Tanao Road
Dinso Road
Maha Chai Road
Baribatra Road
Maha Nak
Chao Phraya River
Phra Lan Road
Bamrung Muang Road
Bamrung Muang Road
Maharat Road
PHRA NAKHON
Sanam Chai Road
Rachini Road
POM PRAP SATTRU PHAI
Rommani Nart Park
Charoen Krung Road
Luang Road
Klong Mon
Ban Mo Road
Ti Thong Road
Krung Kasem Road
Charu Muang Road (Below Expressway)
Si Rat Expressway
041
Arun Amarin Road
Chakkrawat Road
Charoen Krung Road
Wong Wian 22 July
043
Hua Lamphon Railway Station
Phra Pok Klao Bridge
044
SAMPHANTHAWONG
047
Charoen Krung Road
045
046
Hua Lamphong
BANGKOK YAI
Bangkok Yai
Itsaraphap Road
048
050
Somdet Chao Phraya Road
Chao Phraya River
042
Prajadhipok Road
Itsaraphap Road
049
Si Phraya Road
THONBURI
Si Rat Expressway
Phet Kasem Road
Inthara Phitak Road
Lat Ya Road
Charoen Nakhon Road
Surawong R
BAN
RA
Thoet Thai Road
Somdet Phra Chao Tak Sin Road
S8
Krung Thonburi Road
S7
Pho Nimit
Wongwian Yai
Krung Thon Buri
King Taksin Bridge
Ratchaphruek Road
S9
S6
Saphan Taksin
Surasak Road
S5
Surasak
KHLONG SAN
051
Charoen Nakhon Road
Charoen Krung Road
Si Rat Expressway
0
1 km

PHAYA THAI
DIN DAENG
RATCHATHEWI
PATHUM WAN
SATHON
Ari
Sanam Pao
Victory Monument
Phaya Thai
Ratchaprarop
Ratchathewi
Phetchaburi
National Stadium
Siam
Chit Lom
Phloen Chit
Nana
Asok
Ratchadamri
Sam Yan
Si Lom
Sala Daeng
Lumphini
Khong Toei
Queen Sirikit National Conv. Centre
Suan Lumphini Lake
Lumphini Park
Lake Ratchada
Si Rat Expressway
Don Mueang Tollway
Phahon Yothin Road
Soi Ari Samphan
Rama VI Road
Thoet Damri Road
Vibhavadi Rangsit Road
Mit Maitri Road
Soi Phahon Yothin 2
Ratchawithi Road
Soi Ratchawithi
Yothi Road
Rang Nam Road
Phayathai Road
Ratchaprarop Road
Din Daeng Road
Don Pracha Songkhro
Pracha Songkhro 2
Samsen
Si Ayutthaya Road
Chaloem Maha Nakhon Expressway
Phet Buri Road
Asok Din Daeng Road
Ratchadamri Road
Witthayu Road
Phloen Chit Road
Soi Sukhumvit 3
Soi Sukhumvit 13
Soi Sukhumvit 21
Sukhumvit Road
Soi Sukhumvit 4
Soi Ruam Ruedi
Soi Lang Suan
Henri Dunant Road
Sarasin Road
Soi Sukhumvit 16
Ratchadaphisek Road
Soi Plukchit
Rama IV Road
Silom Road
Sathon Tai Road
Soi Suan Phlu
Naradhiwas Rajanagarindra Road
Nang Lychee Road
Yen Akat Road
Rama III Road
Sunthon Kosa Road
W1
CEN
E1
E2
E3
E4
S1
S2
S3
N1
N2
N3
N4
N5

Siriraj Hospital 039 A

Location Phran Nok Road, Siriraj
Architects Luang Wisansilapakam, Professor Mom Chao Wothayakon Worawan
Owner/proprietor Siriraj Hospital
Construction period Waterside Pavilion: 1923; Ratchaphaettayalai: 1952
Conservation award 2006

Siriraj Hospital, Thailand's first medical institution, was conceived by the gracious kindness of His Majesty King Chulalongkorn (Rama V). At present, Siriraj Hospital is crowded with new buildings built to serve the ever-increasing number of patients. Therefore, many old buildings were demolished and changes made to the original site. Nevertheless, some of the original buildings still exist and have been well conserved, bearing testimony to the hospital's long existence. One of these historic buildings is Sala Tha Nam (Waterside Pavilion), an old building that has become a prominent symbol of Siriraj. It was originally a pier that served people who travelled across the river by ferry – especially before 1932, when the hospital was accessible only by water route. Another historic building is the Ratchaphaetthayalai Conference Hall, built following the sixtieth anniversary of Siriraj Hospital.

≈ Wat Rakhang Khositaram, Scripture Hall 040 A

Location Wat Rakhang Khositaram, Arun Amarin Road, Bangkok Noi
Architect/designer Unknown
Owner/proprietor Wat Rakhang Khositaram
Construction period King Rama I period
Conservation award 1987

Wat Rakhang Khositaram (Wat Bangwayai) is an ancient temple which was founded in the Ayutthaya period. It was established as a royal temple under the reign of King Taksin the Great. During King Rama I's reign in the Ratanakosin period, a pond was excavated for the construction of a scriptures hall. During the excavation, a bell was discovered which played a fine tune. The King decided to place it on to the bell tower at Wat Phrasrirattana Satsadaram (The Emerald Temple), and built four new bells to replace the one discovered at the construction site. At the same time, he chose to rename the temple Wat Rakhang Khositaram. Ho Phra Traipidok, the scriptures hall at Wat Rakhang Khositaram, was originally a residence of King Rama I. It was situated to the west of the old *ubosatha* and is a clear example of Thai architecture, comprising three buildings with a fenced deck at the front. The buildings are finely decorated with intricate woodcarvings, coloured glass mosaics and gold leaves, while the interior walls are richly adorned with mural paintings dating back to the period of King Rama I. Beautiful art objects and the scriptures cabinet made of washed gilded lacquer are housed within the hall. The latest restoration was carried out in the year 1982 during the Bangkok Bicentennial Ceremony.

Royal Thai Navy Headquarters 041 A

Location Arun Amarin Road
Owner/proprietor Royal Thai Navy
Construction period 1768
Conservation award 1994

Phra Ratchawang Doem Krung Thonburi (Old Palace of Thonburi) was the royal palace of King Taksin the Great, who established the capital of Thonburi and the palace in 1768. The palace complex comprises buildings combining fine architecture and craftsmanship as befitting a royal residence. The buildings have now been rehabilitated – for instance, at Phra Tamnak Keng Khu there are exhibitions on the life and deeds of King Taksin the Great. King Pinklao Pavilion houses exhibitions on the King and a library, while the ground floor exhibits ancient currencies and pottery.

« Khunluang Rithnarongron House Museum 042 A

Location Tha Pra, Bangkokyai
Architect Unknown
Owner/proprietor Rithnarongron School
Construction period 1923
Conservation award 2010

Khunluang Rithnarongron House Museum is a two-storey building with European architectural influences. It is composed of geometric shapes. The interior is divided into three sections: a reception hall and building wings on the left and right. The reception hall has a square shape. The front of the left wing is divided into two small rooms with a porch consisting of supporting columns for the extended floor of the second storey. On the left is a veranda that continues from the front to the rear of the building, where a back porch is folded up in the middle to provide an entrance from the rear, followed by a semicircular veranda. On the right wing is an elongated hallway that used to be a sermon hall. Today it is a classroom where traditional Thai music is taught. At the front of the right wing is another veranda with a spiral staircase on the rear. This is attached to the curved wall and continues to the second storey. The special feature of this spiral staircase is that it was constructed with a load-bearing wall without a column. Above the stairs are tall windows to allow natural light and cross-ventilation to enter the building. The upper floor is also divided into three sections. The front is a porch overlooking the oval-shaped yard, surrounded by Chinese porcelain. There is another porch located on the rear which is used for services. The museum has currently been registered under the Department of Fine Arts.

« **Santa Cruz Church** 043 A

Location 112 Soi Kudichin, Tesaban Sai 1 Road, Wat Kalaya, Thon buri
Architect Gulielmo Kihn Da Cruz
Owner/proprietor Wat Santa Cruz
Construction period 1913–1916
Conservation award 1999

Santa Cruz Church was built in the year 1767 by Father Corre on the land given by King Taksin the Great. Later, in 1900, the abbot, Father Gulielmo Kihn Da Cruz considered building a new church to replace the old one that was much decayed. Thus, the new church was built between 1913 and 1916. It is said that the abbot himself designed the church with Father Perro and an Italian architect as his assistance. The architecture is renaissance revival in style. At the front, there is an arch and octagonal dome with a cross on the top, decorated with stained glass and stucco. A major restoration was carried out in 1996 to celebrate the anniversary of Santa Cruz Church.

↱ **The Shrine of Kian Un Kong** 044 A

Location Wat Kanlaya, Thonburi
Owner Bud Phisittathapon Simasatien
Construction period King Rama III period
Conservation award 2008

It is widely believed that the shrine was built by Phra Chao Tangsin Maharat's Chinese entourage who settled on Bangluang Canal or the eastern Bangkok Yai Canal while His Majesty established Thonburi as the capital. King Rama I then founded the new capital in Phra Nakhon and the Chinese moved there. Two shrines were neglected to such an extent that they became dilapidated. Afterwards Chao Phra Ya Nikornbadin, one of the first ancestors of the Kanlayahnamit family, donated a plot of land to build Wat Kanlayahnamit in 1825. The Hokkien Chinese, who were the ancestors of Tantiwat's and Simasatien's families, came to pay respect to these shrines. They subsequently reconstructed the shrines with Chinese architecture in the Cheng Dynasty style. That is to say, they have been decorated with many wall paintings, stucco and meticulously carved wooden adornments. The Guan Im statue (a *bodhisattra*) has been installed in the new shrine.

» **Paulinain Brain-Based Learning Centre** 045 A

Location 146 Thatsaban Sai 1 Road, Wat Kanlaya, Thonburi
Owner Phakinee St. Paul de Chatthra
Construction period 1918
Conservation award 2008

Santa Cruz Convent School was founded in 1906 by a supreme patriarch named Louisway, who in turn appointed Phakinee St. Paul de Chatthra to direct it. The school was formerly located on Chaophraya Riverside in Wat Kanlaya, Thonburi. Initially, the school only provided courses in French, English and handicrafts. There were only thirty male and female students, a rather sparse number. Afterwards, the school gradually became more successful and grew in numbers. It moved to its present location in 1918. The first school building was three storeys in height. The school was temporarily closed during the Second World War (1941–1944), although it eventually reopened once the war ended. In 1942, a devastating flood destroyed the 100 Years Memorial Building. For this reason, the school had to be restored, a process which lasted many years. At present, the building serves as the learning centre of Santa Cruz Convent School.

Phra Boromthat Maha Chedi (The Great Pagoda), Wat Prayurawongsawasworawihan

046 A

Location Prachathipok Road, Wat Kanlaya, Thonburi
Owner/proprietor Wat Prayurawonsawas
Construction period 1828
Conservation award 2010

Wat Prayurasawasworawihan is a royal monastery built by Somdej Chao Phraya Borom Maha Prayusawas – the minister in charge of the Royal Treasury during King Rama IV's reign – who sacrificed his coffee plantation to be able to construct the monastery (the site was originally home to it). The edifice was declared a royal monastery by King Rama III and was given the name Wat Prayurawongsawas. It is often referred to as Wat Rue Lek ("Iron-fenced Monastery") owing to its red iron fence. The fence has an arched entrance along its length. Its tips are constructed with lances, swords and axes. At the gate of Phra Boromthat Maha Chedi (The Great Pagoda) is a multi-purpose hall called Parindara Pariyattitham Sala. The hall was originally used by monks and novices for studying the Dharma. In 1916, the hall became the first public library in Thailand. It was later restored as a museum for housing Buddha images.

The Princess Mother Memorial Park 047 A

Location Soi Somdej Chao Phraya 3
Architect Nond-Truengjai Architects Planners Co., Ltd.
Proprietor Chaipattana Foundation
Construction period 1994
Architectural design award 2008

The Princess Mother Memorial Park was the residence of Chao Phraya Sripipatrattanakosatibbhodi (Pear Boonnak), Deputy Director at the Ministry of Finance during King Rama V's reign. The two two-storey buildings are made of concrete and wood-framed structures and are located parallel to each other. They showcase an architectural style typical of the period of King Rama V. On the left of the main buildings is a two-storey building with Chinese influences which reflects the architecture typical of King Rama III's reign. Later, in 1994, some of the ruined raw houses were preserved in their original forms, while others were renovated to form a museum. The renovated raw houses have their roof section elevated to be used as foyers. These foyers are connected to all spaces throughout the building. Several wall openings have been adjusted to let in natural light and establish a connection with the exterior environment. The building also uses materials and colours to incorporate it within the context of the site. Trees, the original gateway and the old well have been preserved in their original state to reflect an old way of life and awaken a sense of nostalgia.

» Wanglee Residence 048 A

Location End of Chiang Mai Road, Khlong San
Architect/designer Unknown
Owner/proprietor Chalant Wanglee
Construction period 1881
Conservation award 1984

Wanglee residence is a two-storey building facing the Chao Phraya River showcasing a Chinese architectural style. Its plan is U-shaped and encloses a courtyard. The ornamentation includes fretwork, mosaics, and stucco of Chinese design. There are also outbuildings, such as the Thai kitchen, the Western kitchen and a servant's house – in addition to a side and back garden. Another building in the compound is a multi-family home with Chinese architectural influences: a large U-shaped building also facing the river. This building was home to the Wanglee family, who used to rent it from Chunking Kneeing Phisonsombatboribun (Phisalbut) before purchasing it from her in 1919. Mr Tan then married Miss Nu, a lady from the Posayanont family. After their marriage, he bought a piece of land in the vicinity of the shop and had a house built here in 1881 which is based on the design of the Posayanont family home. The house has been conserved and maintained with pride up to the present day.

» Somdet Chaophraya Institute of Psychiatry Museum 049 A

Location Somdet Chaophaya Road
Owner/proprietor Somdet Chaopraya Institute of Psychiatry
Construction period Late King Rama IV to the early King Rama V period
Conservation award 1987

Somdet Chaopraya Institute of Psychiatry Museum is a two-storey edifice built in a romantic style with English Tudor and Moorish influences. The building faces the north with a tower on the northwestern corner. Originally, the house belonged to Chao Phraya Surawongwaiyawat. When King Rama V wished to improve the asylum at Pak Klong San, more land was bought and

the building was subsequently expanded. The psychiatric hospital was thus founded which has developed into the present-day Somdet Chaophraya Institute of Psychiatry. From 1981 to 1982, the house underwent a major restoration by the Fine Arts Department and was registered as a heritage building in 1985. The building has been reinhabited to house reception halls on the ground floor and a museum on the upper floor. In front of the house is the monument of Professor Dr Fon Sangsingkaew, regarded by many to be the father of psychiatry in Thailand.

Ubosatha,
Wat Thong Nophakhun, 050 A

Location Wat Thong Nophakhun, 4645 Khlong San
Architect/designer Unknown
Owner/proprietor Wat Thong Nophakhun
Construction period King Rama III period
Conservation award 1982

Wat Thong Nophakhun was founded in the late Ayutthaya period, as indicated by the Ayutthaya-style pagodas with indented corners. During the reign of King Rama III, Phraya Choduekratchasetthi restored the building and dedicated it to the King; the temple was thereby reestablished as a royal temple. Later, during the reign of King Rama IV, the style of the *ubosatha* shifted from the Chinese style, which was favoured by the former reign, to a traditional Thai style, complete with a Thai roof decorated with gable ends. The porch was also expanded to support the roof. The most distinguishable and unique feature of the *ubosatha* is the ellipse-shaped windows that are derived from the shape of the monks' ceremonial fan, flanking the crowned window in the middle. The interior is decorated with various mural paintings by the abbot Phra Khru Kasinsangwon, depicting scenes from Vessantara Jataka. There are also Chinese tables and a large curtain is hung on the wall behind the image of Buddha.

Tamnak Phra Chao Suea (Golden Pavilion) Wat Sai

051 A

Location Wat Sai, Bang Khun Thian, Chom Thong, Bangkok
Architect/designer Unknown
Owner/proprietor Wat Sai
Construction period Ayutthaya period
Conservation award 2004

Tamnak Phra Chao Suea, or Tamnak Thong (Golden Pavilion), is built in a traditional Thai style. It is made of teakwood on high stilts and dates back to the Ayutthaya period, approximately 300 years ago. The original decorations were gilded lacquer works, but almost all of these have decayed or faded over time; only the gilded decorations on the interior partitions still remain in an almost complete state. The interior of the building is divided into rooms believed to be the King's bedroom and private chambers. The bedroom is decorated with false windows whose frames are elaborately carved and gilded in designs depicting the feet of lions and many other beautiful motifs; however, these are partly deteriorated because of their age. The pavilion has a gable roof which is tiled and decorated at the top with stucco depicting a Garuda. The gable ends are designed in the shape of Nagas. The design is finished with a lower-tier hipped roof. Tamnak Thong was used as a scriptures hall for a period of time; however, the pavilion is currently not being used. It has been registered as a national monument since the year 1962.

District of Power and Politics

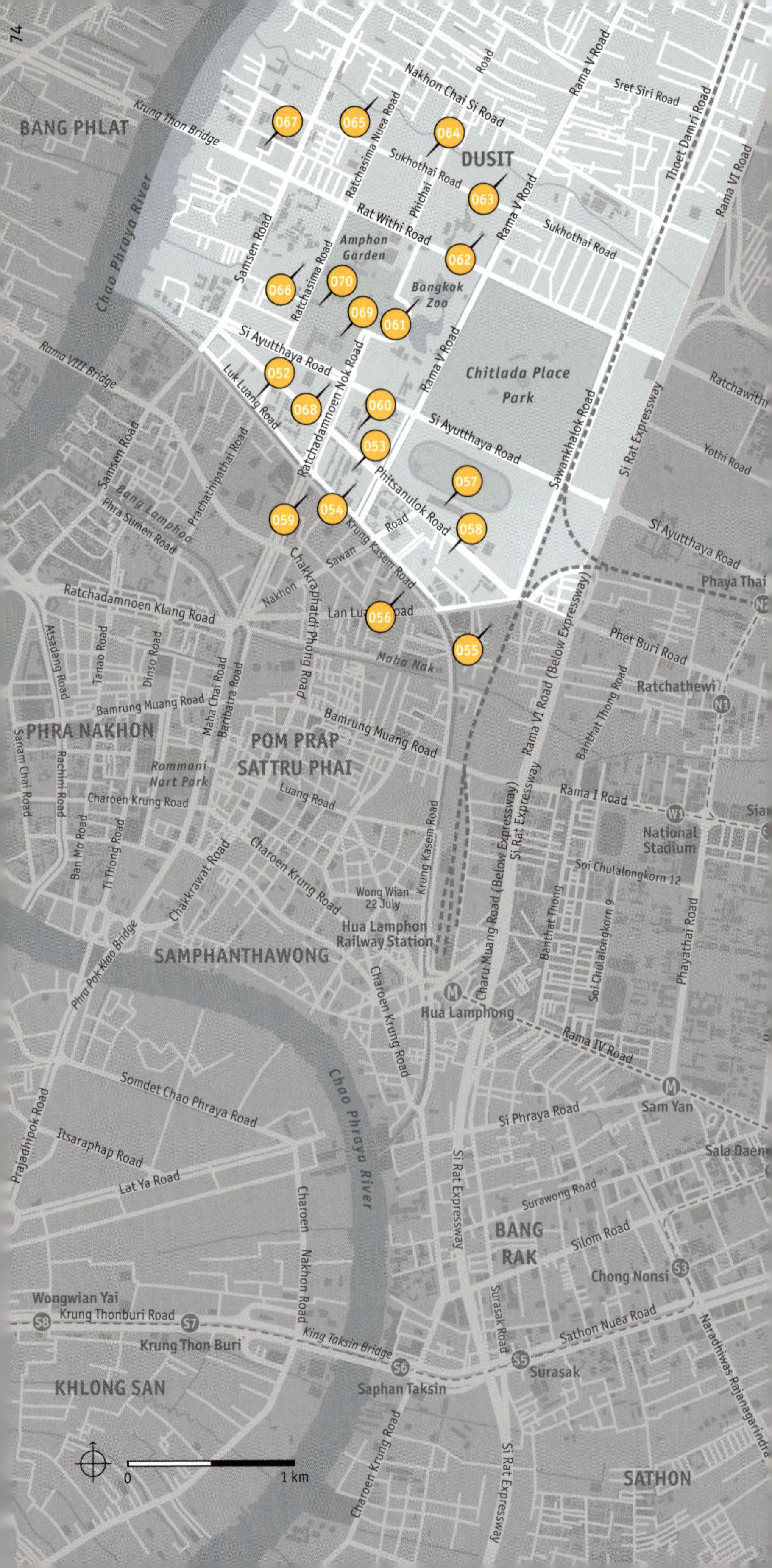
BANG PHLAT
Krung Thon Bridge
Chao Phraya River
067
065
064
DUSIT
063
062
061
066
070
069
052
068
060
053
057
058
059
054
056
055
Nakhon Chai Si Road
Ratchasima Nuea Road
Sukhothai Road
Sret Siri Road
Rama V Road
Thoet Damri Road
Rama VI Road
Phichai
Rat Withi Road
Amphon Garden
Samsen Road
Ratchasima Road
Bangkok Zoo
Sukhothai Road
Si Ayutthaya Road
Rama VIII Bridge
Luk Luang Road
Ratchadamnoen Nok Road
Chitlada Place Park
Sawankhalok Road
Si Rat Expressway
Ratchawithi
Yothi Road
Phitsanulok Road
Samsen Road
Prachathipathai Road
Bang Lamphoo
Phra Sumen Road
Krung Kasem Road
Chakkraphatdi Phong Road
Nakhon Sawan Road
Si Ayutthaya Road
Phaya Thai
N2
Ratchadamnoen Klang Road
Lan Luang Road
Maha Nak
Phet Buri Road
Ratchathewi
N1
Atsadang Road
Tanao Road
Dinso Road
Maha Chai Road
Baribatra Road
Bamrung Muang Road
Rama VI Road (Below Expressway)
Banthat Thong Road
PHRA NAKHON
POM PRAP SATTRU PHAI
Bamrung Muang Road
Sanam Chai Road
Rachini Road
Rommani Nart Park
Charoen Krung Road
Luang Road
Krung Kasem Road
Charu Muang Road (Below Expressway)
Si Rat Expressway
Rama I Road
W1
National Stadium
Ban Mo Road
Ti Thong Road
Chakkrawat Road
Charoen Krung Road
Wong Wian 22 July
Soi Chulalongkorn 12
Hua Lamphon Railway Station
Banthat Thong
Soi Chulalongkorn 9
Phayathai Road
SAMPHANTHAWONG
Phra Pok Klao Bridge
Charoen Krung Road
Hua Lamphong
Rama IV Road
Chao Phraya River
Somdet Chao Phraya Road
Sam Yan
Prajadhipok Road
Itsaraphap Road
Si Phraya Road
Lat Ya Road
Charoen Nakhon Road
Si Rat Expressway
Sala Daeng
Surawong Road
BANG RAK
Silom Road
Chong Nonsi
S3
Wongwian Yai
Krung Thonburi Road
S8
S7
Surasak Road
Sathon Nuea Road
Narathiwas Rajanagarindra
Krung Thon Buri
King Taksin Bridge
S5
Surasak
S6
KHLONG SAN
Saphan Taksin
Charoen Krung Road
Si Rat Expressway
0
1 km
SATHON

PHAYA THAI
DIN DAENG
HUAI KHWANG
WATTHANA
KHLONG TOEI
Ari
Sanam Pao
Phahon Yothin Road
Soi Phahon Yothin 2
Vibhavadi Rangsit Road
Mit Maitri Road
Don Mueang Tollway
Pracha Songkhro Road
Soi Pracha Suk
Ratchadaphisek Road
Thailand Cultural Centre
Soi Ratchawithi
Expressway
Din Daeng Road
Don Pracha Songkhro
Pracha Songkhro 2
Samsen
Watthanatham Road
Ratchaprarop Road
Chaloem Maha Nakhon Expressway
Phra Ram 9
Rama IX Road
Si Rat Expressway
Samsen Nai
Asok Din Daeng Road
Ratchaprarop
Phet Buri Road
Phetchaburi
Saen Saep
Ratchadamri Road
Witthayu Road
Soi Sukhumvit 3
Soi Sukhumvit 13
Soi Sukhumvit 21
Chit Lom
Phloen Chit Road
Phloen Chit
Soi Lang Suan
Soi Ruam Ruedi
Soi Sukhumvit 4
Nana
Sukhumvit Road
Asok
Sukhumvit
Soi Sukhumvit 49
Ratchadamri
Sarasin Road
Lumphini Park
Lumphini Lake
Soi Sukhumvit 16
Soi Sukhumvit 22
Soi Sukhumvit 39
Phrom Phong
Lake Ratchada
Soi Plukchit
Rama IV Road
Lumphini
Soi Sukhumvit 24
Soi Sukhumvit 26
Soi Sukhumvit 36
Khong Toei
Queen Sirikit National Conv. Centre
Thang Rot Fai Sai Kao Road
Sunthon Kosa Road
Yen Akat Road
Nang Lynchee Road
Rama III Road

≈ The Crown Property Bureau 052 A

Location 173 Ratchasima Road
Architect/designer Unknown
Owner/proprietor Crown Property Bureau
Construction period King Rama V period
Conservation award 1982

The Crown Property Bureau was the former residence of Prince Krommaluang Lopburiramet, son of King Rama V and Phra Wimadathoe Krommaphra Sutthasininat. The King ordered the palace be built for the Prince and named it Wang Ladawan after the Prince's grandfather, Krommamuen Phumintharaphakdi (Prince Ladawan). The palace is often referred to as *Wang Deang*. Prince Krommaluang Lopburiramet lived at this palace until he passed away in 1932. The property was then sold to the Crown Property Bureau in 1945, after the Second World War. Later, the Bureau restored the building and have used it as their headquarters right up until the present day. The two-storey palace is in a renaissance revival architectural style with a three-storey high tower on the right wing. The roof is hipped with monier tiles imported from France. The ground floor walls are rusticated, while the walls of the first floor are plain and decorated with stucco. The interior is also adorned with Chinese decorative art, which is evidenced by the mural paintings, woodcarvings, wrought iron and hanging lanterns.

Thai Khu Fa Building (Government House) 053 A

Location Phitsanulok Road, Dusit
Architect Mario Tamagno and Annibale Rigotti (extension), Silpa Bhirasri (Corrado Feroci)
Owner Secretariat of the Prime Minister
Construction period 1926
Conservation award 1989

Thai Khu Fa Building was originally named the Kraison Building after Prince Krommaluang Raksaronres (Prince Kraison), the first person who acquired Phuengbun de Ayuthaya. The building is the principal structure of Ban Norasing, the residence of General Chaophraya Ramrakhop (Mom Luang Fuea Phuengbun). It is an example of a Venetian gothic revival architecture, evoking the Palazzo Ca' d'Oro in Venice with its dome, pointed arch, tower, elaborate mouldings and stucco ornamentation. The building is currently used as the Prime Minister's office and reception house. The last building restoration took place in 2003.

≈ Nari Samoson and Saeng Athit Buildings

054 A

Location Government House, Nakhon Pathom Road
Architect/designer Unknown
Proprietor Office of the Prime Minister
Construction period King Rama VI period
Conservation award 2005

The government house was originally called Baan Norasing – a noble residence built by order of King Rama VI to be given to Admiral Chao Phraya Ramrakhop (Mom Luang Fuea Phuengbun), who was the viceroy of the royal household. The government bought the house at a later period so that it could be used as the office of the Prime Minister, a role it has fulfilled ever since 1963. Nari Samoson Building is a single-storey office building boasting an eclectic design. It was originally called Tuek Phra Khan. The building's notable feature is the mixture of various architectural elements that it brings together in its design. Saeng Athit Building is situated to the south of Nari Samoson Building. It was originally a staircase hall that linked a group of buildings together in the house. Over the course of time, the connecting corridors were removed and adjacent buildings demolished. This building is also an example of eclectic architecture.

≽ Manangkhasila Mansion 055 A

Location Lan Luang Road, Dusit
Architect/designer Edward Healey
Owner/proprietor The Treasury Department
Construction period King Rama VI period
Conservation award 2002

Manangkhasila Mansion was built during the reign of King Rama VI on the land that he gave to Phraya Udomratchaphakdi (Tho Sucharitkul). He named the house Baan Manangkhasila. The design for the building was clearly influenced by Tudor architecture which is evidenced by the wood-battened walls, the half-timber structure, the high-pitched roofs intricately decorated with dormers and gables, the wooden mouldings and the Tudor arches. In 1952, the house ownership was transferred to the Bank of Asia. The government borrowed the building so that it could be used as a reception house and as the headquarters for the Seri Manangkhasila political party. In 1960, it was bought by the Bank of Thailand to be given to the Ministry of Finance as an exchange for continuing the use of Wang Bang Kuhn Prom. Since then, the property has been used by several government offices. As of 1975, it has been used as the house of the National Council of Women of Thailand under the Royal Patronage of Her Majesty the Queen.

≽ Suriyanuwat Building 056 A

Location Krung Kasem Road
Architect/designer Mario Tamagno
Owner/proprietor National Economic and Social Development Board
Construction period 1906–1908
Conservation award 1993

Suriyanuwat Building combines hip and gable roofs with dormers. The ornamentation includes European-inspired fretwork and stucco. The building was originally the home of Maha Ammat-ek Phrya Suriyanuwat (Koed Bunnag) – the first economist of Thailand who wrote *Sappayasat* (*Economic Science*). In 1950, the National Economic and Social Council bought the house so that they could use it as their permanent base. At present, it functions as offices for high officials of the National Economic and Social Development Board, a reception house and an exhibition hall displaying personal belongings of Maha Ammat-ek Phrya Suriyanuwat.

» Multi-purpose Auditorium, Royal Turf Club of Thailand 057 A

Location 183 Phitsanulok Road
Architect/designer Unknown
Owner Royal Turf Club of Thailand under the Royal Patronage of HM the King
Construction period 1916
Conservation award 1984

The horse racing venue, which was built during the reign King Rama VI, is named the Royal Turf Club of Thailand. The multi-purpose hall was originally the royal stable of King Rama VI. It is a rectangular building with a large hall in the middle flanked by the entrance to the south and the observation hall – where the King once sat to watch the races – located to the north. It boasts a neo-classical architecture beautifully decorated with stucco, mouldings and wood awning windows. The middle hall is worthy of note owing to its steel tied truss roof structure covering the whole area, without middle supports. At present, the hall is used to accommodate badminton courts, while the floor has been elevated by approximately 80 cm. It is assumable from structure and design, however, that this might not have been a stable as was generally believed, but rather an indoor arena to practise dressage riding.

» Phitsanulok Mansion 058 A

Location 426–428 Phitsanulok Rd
Architects Mario Tamagno and Annibale Rigotti
Owner Bureau of the Crown Property
Construction period 1923
Conservation award 2002

Phitsanulok Mansion, originally named Baan Banthomsin, was built under the initiation of King Rama VI as a residence for Major General Phraya Anirutthewa. The three-storey principal building, or Tuek Yai, is an example of Venetian gothic revival architecture featuring an underground floor. Several parts of the roof structure display a dome and deck. The building is decorated with stucco and intricate woodcarvings. In front of the building there stands a sculpture of Narai Banthomsin (Vishnu Lying on the Sea of Milk) given by King Rama IV, from which the house's name was derived. The compound boasts an English-style landscape. In late 1942, during the First World War, Phraya Anirutthewa and his family moved to Wat Tam Nak Near. The Bureau of the Crown Property bought the main building for use as a government reception house. Today the building is used as the Prime Minister's residence.

︽ The Royal Thai Army Headquarters 059 A

Location Ratchadamnoen Nok Road
Architect/designer Unknown
Owner/proprietor Royal Thai Army
Construction period 1909
Conservation award 1987

The Royal Thai Army Headquarters were originally built in the year 1909 as a military school. King Rama V presided over the opening ceremony which took place on 25 December 1909. The two-storey building is an example of a neo-Palladian architecture, featuring a hipped roof which is accentuated by a three-storey porch in the middle of the front façade. The porch has a gable roof decorated with the emblem of King Rama V on the pediment. Each storey of the porch comprises three arches alternating with superimposed pilasters. The walls are set behind the arches. Since the Military School moved to Khao Cha-ngok, the building is now used as the Royal Thai Army Headquarters.

» Mathayom Wat Benjamabopit School 060 A

Location Si Ayutthaya Road
Owner/proprietor Mathayom Wat Benchamabophit School
Construction period 1902
Conservation award 1984

Mathayom Wat Benchamabophit School is an example of a renaissance revival architecture with a symmetrical plan and a hipped roof with three porches. The middle porch is gabled and accentuated by a fractable, upon which is inscribed a record of the construction. The rusticated ground floor walls feature rectangular windows, whereas the first floor windows are arched. Taken as a whole, the decorative elements are strong, systematic, and applied with repeated rhythm to achieve a steady and firm appearance. This may be interpreted as a Western-influenced architectural characteristic, typical of the King Rama V period. The building is painted in a striking shade of mauve.

Glass House, Dusit Zoo 061 A

Location Dusit Zoo, Rama V Road
Architect Phraya Borihanratchamanop
Owner The Zoological Park Organisation
Construction period King Rama VII period
Conservation award 2002

This building is part of Dusit Zoo or Khao Din, the first zoological park in Thailand. It was founded during the reign of King Rama V, following his visits to a number of zoos dotted around Europe. The single-storey Glass House has a steel frame hip roof decorated with carved wooden fretwork. The building was originally a wooden framework but an extension made of reinforced concrete was later added. The structure is decorated with stained glass panels and mouldings. The construction of the Glass House was part of the Dusit Zoo development project during the reign of King Rama VII, who assigned Maha Swektri Phraya Borihanratchamanop as project director. In those days, the Glass House was a reception hall for members of the Royal Family. It currently serves as the office of the Director of Dusit Zoo.

≽ Vajiravudh College 062 A

Location 197 Ratchawithi Road
Architect/designer Edward Healey and Phra Samitlekha (first period); Phra Sarotrattananimman and Luang Wisansilapakam (second period)
Owner/proprietor Vajiravudh College
Construction period 1915–1917, 1932
Conservation award 1982

Vajiravudh College was originally called Mahadlek College and was founded under the initiation of King Rama VI. At that time, the school comprised wooden buildings with a thatched roof. Later, the first permanent buildings were constructed: four college buildings and the conference hall. King Rama VI instructed that the design concept was to follow the architecture of Thailand in order to harmonise with Wat Benchamabophi, located on the opposite side of Dusit Zoo. These multi-storey buildings are ranked amongst the first of their kind to apply this architectural style. In 1926, during the reign of King Rama VII, the world faced a great economic downturn; in order to save the budget, the King ordered Ratchawitthayalai School to be relocated and merged with Mahadlek College. It was then given its current title. The extension to the school heralded the second construction period. Vajuramongkut Building and a health centre were built in 1931 and completed in 1932. The buildings display the same style as those from the first construction period.

≈ Varichwes Palace 063 A

Location Sukhothai Road, Dusit
Architect Phra Sarotratthananimman
Owner/proprietor Matching Studio Public Co., Ltd.
Construction period 1933
Conservation award 2008

Varichwes Palace was the former residence of Her Royal Highness Princess Wapeebussabahkorn, daughter of King Chulalongkorn (King Rama V). It was one of the buildings constructed at a notable turning point in architecture. At the end of the reign of King Rama VII, Thai architecture was influenced by ancient Western architecture, but, on the other hand, at the beginning of the reign of King Rama VIII it had started to showcase a more modern and international style. Construction was based on simplicity and cost-effectiveness due to the economic depression. Building materials changed from natural materials to durable and permanent ones; for instance, reinforced concrete was used instead of wood. Also, both the structure and the decorative elements were adorned with geometrical designs instead of old perforated patterns. It was not only the turning point of an architectural epoch, but for architects too; that it to say, previously architects had been members of the royal family, noblemen and foreigners but now, by stark contrast, they too were ordinary people.

Tamnak Princess Apphantripacha 064 A

Location 1 Phichai Road, Dusit
Architect/designer Unknown
Owner/proprietor Crown Property Bureau
Construction period 1897–1927
Conservation award 1999

Tamnak Princess Apphantripacha is a two-storey brick masonry building built in a colonial style. It has a hipped roof and wooden louvres for ventilation. The house is surrounded by corridors and decorated with wooden fretwork in foliage designs at the clerestories between rooms. The location of this building was originally the palace of Princess Apphantripacha, the daughter of King Rama V. After the princess passed away, the rights of property were divided among several ownerships. The area was once used as a school which was given the name Kattiyaniphadung. After the school closed down, the present owner, the Crown Property Bureau, rented it to the Chart Thai political party to be used as the Party's office. The Party quickly realised the value of the building; it has thus been conserved to be used as a library and reception house for the benefit of their VIP guests.

≈ Suan Parichat 065 A

Location Rachasima Road, Dusit
Architects Plan Architects Co., Ltd.
Owner/proprietor Parichat Company
Construction period 1981
Architectural design award 1982

The Suan Parichat project is an apartment complex which was designed to emphasise the uniqueness of Thai culture and the lifestyle in which Thai people previously relied upon as part of living next to rivers and canals. The architecture combines a Thai traditional house with modern technologies. Each compound comprises two apartment units. The balconies on the second floor of each apartment are on the same level and connected in such a way that they divide the open space. On the ground floor there are non-load-bearing columns, glazed walls and a terrace to accentuate the elevated floor of the traditional Thai house. Roads are located at the back of the compound. There is an open space used as a communal area on the edge of the canal.

« Arts and Cultural Centre, Suan Dusit Rajabhat University 066 A

Location 295 Ratchasima Road
Architect Chaophraya Yomaraj (Pan Sukhum)
Owner Rajabhat Institute Suan Dusit
Construction period ca. 1911–1913
Conservation award 1994

Tamnak Yaowapha is a two-storey elevated building which is structured with a concrete and teak wood frame. It has a high-pitched roof which originally consisted of cement tiles, although these were later replaced by red monier ones. The interior is divided into clusters of living quarters, similar to an apartment. The building used to be the residence of three princesses who were daughters of King Rama V:

namely, Princess Yaowaphaphongsanit, Princess Praphaphanphilai and Princess Wapibusabakorn. After democratisation, Suan Sunantha became an academic institute. *Tamnak Yaowapha* currently serves as the centre for the institute's cultural activities and has fulfilled this role since the year 1989.

» Dusit Samoson (Phraya Prasertsuphakit Residence) 067 A

Location 123 Ratchawithi Road, Wachiraphayaban
Architect/designer Annibale Rigotti and Mario Tamagno
Owner/proprietor Dusit Avenue Juristic Condominium
Construction period 1905–1913
Conservation award 1982

The residence of Phraya Prasertsuphakit (Phoem Krairoek) is built in the Arts and Crafts style, albeit combined with several classical elements. The building consists of a two-storey structure with a car drop-off porch situated at the front. The building has a hipped roof with dormers, segmental arched windows, stucco mouldings and woodcarving ornamentation. Façades are painted a cream shade of white. An octagonal porch is situated at the western part and the deck is to the east which is reached by a spiral staircase inside the house. The house had been used as a residence prior to 1997 when it was renovated to form part of Dusit Avenue Juristic Condominium. It now houses a a multipurpose hall, a meeting room and a meditation room on the upper floor.

⩯ Parutsakawan Palace 068 A

Location Junction of Si Ayutthaya and Ratchadamnoen Road
Architect Mario Tamagno
Owner/proprietor National Intelligence Agency and the Royal Thai Police
Construction period 1903
Conservation award 1989

Wang Parutsakawan comprises two important buildings. The first, Phra Tamnak Suan Parutsakawan, was built under the initiation of King Rama V as a residence for Field Marshal Prince Phitsanulok Prachanat. The building is an example of a romantic architecture. It originally had two storeys although, later, another storey was added. On the ground floor there is a grand reception hall, a guest room, a dining room and an apartment for guests. The second and third floors serve as the private quarters for the owner. The other building is Suan Chitrlada Pavilion which formerly belonged to King Rama VI before his ascension to the throne. Later, he bequeathed it to Prince Phitsanulok Prachanat in exchange for his land at Wasukri Pier. The two-storey building is an example of Stile Liberty, or German Art Nouveau architecture, beautifully decorated with stucco. The roof is a combination of several hipped roofs and windows covered with arched canopies, fitted with fretwork. In addition to its elaborate ornamentation, the building is also designed with a drop-off porch for cars. After Thailand's democratisation in 1932, the government expropriated the palace and converted it into office space. Today, Phra Tamnak Suan Parutsakawan is used as the headquarters of the National Intelligence Agency. Phra Tamnak Suan Chitrlada accommodates the Royal Thai Police Museum.

Royal Amporn Garden Pavilion 069 A

Location Ratchadamneon Nok Road
Architect/designer Casa Co., Ltd.
Owner Bureau of the Royal Household
Construction period 1972
Architectural design award 1984

Royal Amporn Garden Pavilion is a multipurpose building comprising a conference hall, seminar rooms and a badminton court. The highlights of this location are a large fountain at the front leading to an existing building and the King Rama V equestrian monument at the entrance to Ratchadamnoen Nok Road. Owing to the main concept behind the multi-purpose room – i.e. to accommodate a total capacity of 1,000 people – both sides of the room were designed with a free-form terrace. There are visitors' WCs on one side of the stage and a private area for performers on the other, including dressing rooms and WCs. Below the stage is ample storage space. A pantry with a slope leads to a multi-purpose room. The folded-slab roof structure is made of reinforced concrete, with a cantilevered roof design for the terrace. Steel girders and box girder decks provide air duct spaces and are used as passages by lighting staff to the projector room.

≈ Suan Kularb Palace Throne Hall 070 A

Location 14 U Thong Road, Dusit
Architect/designer Mario Tamagno
Proprietor Princess Somsawali Phra Worarachathinaddamat
Construction period 1912
Conservation award 1994

The throne hall of Suan Kularb Palace is a Victorian concert hall in wooden frame construction. Special features of the building are the fresco paintings on the walls. It was originally founded by King Rama V as a contemporary hall on the palace compound and used to be a residence of Admiral Somdet Chaofa Asadangdechawut Krommaluang Nakhon Ratchasima, the Minister of Naval Defence in the reign of King Rama VI. In 1993, the Special Services Department restored the main building, pavilions and walls under supervision of the Fine Arts Department. Today, the hall is part of the royal residence of Princess Somsawali Phra Worarachathinaddamat.

Central Business District

071 Nonthi House

072 Tuek Daeng (Office of the State Railway of Thailand, Yotse)

073 Bangkok Railway Station (Hua Lamphong Railway Station)

074 Jim Thompson House

075 Chulalongkorn University Alumni Association

076 Pharotracha House

077 Maha Chulalongkorn Building (Faculty of Arts Building)

078 Chulalongkorn University Auditorium

079 Queen Saovabha Memorial Institute

080 Lumpini Park Public Library

081 The Royal Bangkok Sports Club Polo Club

082 American Ambassador's Residence

083 Dutch Ambassador's Residence

084 Nai Lert House

085 Spa 1930 (Doll House)

086 Siam Commercial Bank Plc., Thanon Petchaburi Branch

087 Suan Phakkad Palace

088 Makkasan Train Warehouse

089 Xavier Church

090 Phaya Thai Palace

091 Round Building, Mahidol University

092 Thai Military Bank, Sanampao Branch

093 Mekhala Ruchi Pavilion

094 Portuguese Ambassador's Residence

095 O.P. Place

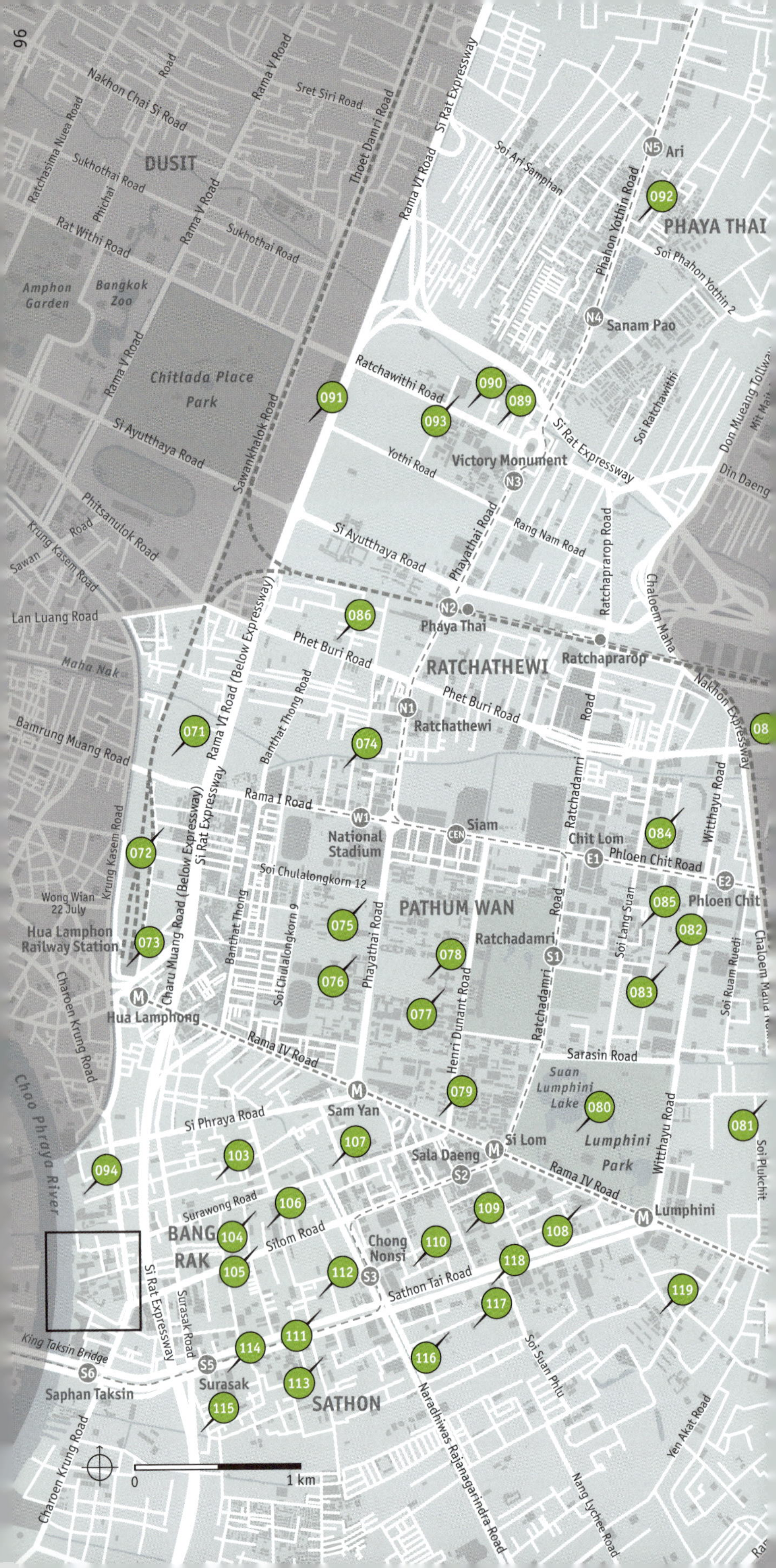
DUSIT
Nakhon Chai Si Road
Road
Rama V Road
Sret Siri Road
Thoet Damri Road
Rama VI Road
Si Rat Expressway
Ratchasima Nuea Road
Sukhothai Road
Phichai
Rama V Road
Rat Withi Road
Sukhothai Road
Amphon Garden
Bangkok Zoo
Chitlada Place Park
Rama V Road
Sawankhalok Road
Si Ayutthaya Road
Phitsanulok Road
Krung Kasem Road
Sawan
Road
Lan Luang Road
Maha Nak
Bamrung Muang Road
Soi Ari Samphan
N5 Ari
Phahon Yothin Road
PHAYA THAI
Soi Phahon Yothin 2
N4 Sanam Pao
Ratchawithi Road
Yothi Road
Victory Monument
N3
Si Rat Expressway
Soi Ratchawithi
Don Mueang Tollway
Din Daeng
Phayathai Road
Rang Nam Road
Ratchaprarop Road
Chalaem Maha Nakhon Expressway
Si Ayutthaya Road
N2 Phaya Thai
Ratchaprarop
Phet Buri Road
RATCHATHEWI
Phet Buri Road
Road
N1 Ratchathewi
Rama VI Road (Below Expressway)
Banthat Thong Road
Rama I Road
W1 National Stadium
CEN Siam
Ratchadamri
Chit Lom
E1 Phloen Chit Road
Witthayu Road
E2 Phloen Chit
Krung Kasem Road
Wong Wian 22 July
Hua Lamphon Railway Station
Charu Muang Road (Below Expressway)
Si Rat Expressway
Soi Chulalongkorn 12
Banthat Thong
Soi Chulalongkorn 9
Phayathai Road
PATHUM WAN
Ratchadamri
Road
S1
Soi Lang Suan
Soi Ruam Ruedi
Henri Dunant Road
Ratchadamri
Charoen Krung Road
M Hua Lamphong
Rama IV Road
Sarasin Road
Suan Lumphini Lake
Lumphini Park
Witthayu Road
Soi Plukchit
Chao Phraya River
Si Phraya Road
M Sam Yan
M Si Lom
Sala Daeng
S2
Rama IV Road
M Lumphini
Surawong Road
BANG RAK
Silom Road
Chong Nonsi
S3
Sathon Tai Road
Si Rat Expressway
Surasak Road
King Taksin Bridge
S6 Saphan Taksin
S5 Surasak
SATHON
Soi Suan Phlu
Naradhiwas Rajanagarindra Road
Yen Akat Road
Nang Lychee Road
Charoen Krung Road
0
1 km
071
072
073
074
075
076
077
078
079
080
081
082
083
084
085
086
089
090
091
092
093
094
103
104
105
106
107
108
109
110
111
112
113
114
115
116
117
118
119

Soi Charoen Krung 36
100
096
095
097
Soi Charoen Krung 40
Charoen Krung Road
101
099
098
102
Soi Charoen Krung 42/1
0
200 m
Don Mueang Tollway
Soi Pracha Suk
Ratchadaphisek Road
Huai Khwang
Road
Pracha
Songkhro
DIN DAENG
Thailand Cultural Centre
Lat Phrao
Ratchadaphisek Road
Watthanatham Road
Thiam Ruam Mit Road
Samsen
Chuat Yai
Phra Ram 9
Rama IX Road
Samsen Nai
Si Rat Expressway
Rama IX Road
Asok Din Daeng Road
Phetchaburi
Royal City Avenue
Saen Saep
Phet Buri Road
Soi Sukhumvit 13
Soi Sukhumvit 21
Soi Sukhumvit 49
Asok
Sukhumvit
Soi Sukhumvit 55
Soi Sukhumvit 63
Sukhumvit Road
Soi Sukhumvit 39
WATTHANA
Ekkamai Soi 22
Soi Sukhumvit 16
Soi Sukhumvit 22
Phrom Phong
Ekkamai Soi 5
Ratchadaphisek Road
Soi Sukhumvit 24
Soi Sukhumvit 26
Soi Sukhumvit 16
Thong Lo
Queen Sirikit National Conv. Centre
KHLONG TOEI
Soi Sukhumvit 36
Ban Kluai Tai Alley
Ekkamai
Rama IV Road
Rama IV Road
Thang Rot Fai Sai Kao Road
Sunthon Kosa Road
Phra Khanong
Maha Nakhon Expressway
Chaloem Maha Nakhon Expressway

Bangkok City of Life
central

≈ Nonthi House 071 B

Location Rama I Road (the corner of Kasatsuek Bridge and Yotse Bridge), Rong Mueang
Architect Ercole Manfredi
Owner/proprietor Ministry of Energy
Construction period 1897
Conservation award 2006

Nonthi House (Baan Nonthi) is an example of classic revival architecture. It was originally constructed around 1897 as a single detached building known as Tuek Klang (Central Building, the main building of the Department of Energy Development and Promotion). The house was given to Phraya Anurakratchamonthian (Mom Ratchawong Pum Malakul) by King Rama V. In 1913, to mark the occasion on which Phraya Anurakratchamonthian was promoted to the title Chao Phraya Thammathikoranathibodi (Minister of the Royal Household), King Rama VI presented him with a sum of money for the extension and landscape design. Therefore, a three-storey building was constructed which was linked to the first building by bridge. The building features beautiful decorative elements encompassing carvings, intricate sculptures and paintings which are mostly influenced by renaissance art. Distinctive elements are the Nonthikan bulls' heads adorning the door frames and other parts of the house – hence the name *Baan Nonthi* – as well as ceilings decorated with floral and fruit designs. Carvings and paintings of Western design depict stories of Thailand involving figures such as Ramayana, Mekhla and Ramasura. In 1959, Nonthi House was assigned to the National Energy Office, or the Department of Energy Development and Promotion. A major restoration was carried out during 2003 and 2004 by the Fine Arts Department.

Tuek Daeng (Office of the State Railway of Thailand, Yotse) 072 B

Location Rong Mueang Road, Pathum Wan
Architect/designer Luang Sukhawat
Owner State Railway of Thailand
Construction period 1928–1931
Conservation award 2006

Tuek Daeng (Red Building) is situated near Saphan Kasatsuek (Kasatsuek Bridge) on the banks of the Phadung Krungkasem Canal. The three-storey building has a U-shaped plan. The northern and southern wings – whose reddish brown appearance owing to the brick masonry is the reason for its well-known name – have two storeys. The building was originally intended to be used as storage. Distinguished architectural features of Tuek Daeng are the exposed structural elements and the brick masonry, lending it a timeless appearance. Its simplicity, stateliness, strength and functionality have made the building a perfect example of modern architecture. Today, the building houses several offices of the State Railway of Thailand. It has been renovated and installed with energy conservation devices to control usage of energy effectively.

≫ Bangkok Railway Station (Hua Lamphong Railway Station) 073 B

Location Rama IV Road, Rong Mueang
Architects Mario Tamagno and Alfredo Rigazzi
Owner State Railway of Thailand
Construction period 1910–1916
Conservation award 2002

Bangkok Railway Station, or Hua Lam Phong Station, comprises the station hall with its wide arched roof and the neo-classical front hall. The front hall is rectangular with a flat roof and a tower at each end, giving the impression that the arched roof of the station hall is flanked by two towers. The building is also praiseworthy as an example of a well-designed and meticulously built steel structure. The construction of the first railway of Thailand, beginning at Hua Lam Phong, was officially opened by King Rama V on 16 July 1891. However, the permanent station hall was built between 1906 and 1912 during King Rama VI's reign, followed by the front hall in 1916. In spite of its continued use and several modifications, the original buildings have been conserved and cherished.

≪ Jim Thompson House 074 B

Location 6 Soi Kasemsant 2, Rama II Road, Pathum Wan
Architect Bunyong Nikhrothanont
Owner James H. W. Thompson Foundation
Construction period 1986
Architectural design award 1996

Jim Thompson House is renowned for its traditional Thai architecture and tranquil tropical garden, a rare sight in the midst of Bangkok. The complex comprises six traditional Thai houses sourced from Bangkok and Ayutthaya. These are grouped together in a spatial sequence to suit Thompson's preferences, who lived here following his retirement from the Office of Strategic Services (OSS) in 1959. Thompson opened his house to visitors in 1964.

The red exteriors are caused by creosote wood preservative. Jim Thompson House has also turned into a tourist hotspot owing to Thompson's extensive art collection. After he disappeared in Malaysia in 1967, the house was commissioned to the James H. W. Thompson Foundation which has carefully maintained the compound.

Chulalongkorn University Alumni Association under the Patronage of His Majesty the King 075 B

Location Phaya Thai Road, Wangmai
Architect/designer Jen Skoltanarak
Owner Chulalongkorn University
Construction period 1967
Conservation award 2010

The overarching aim of the Chulalongkorn University Alumni Association under the patronage of His Majesty the King was to establish and maintain a sense of unity between alumni and current students by providing facilities for sports, entertainment and educational resources, promoting knowledge-sharing networks and honouring members who have rendered distinguished services to the association. It was established in the year 1946, governed by His Royal Highness Prince Vanna Vaidhayakara as first president. During the first two years, board meetings took place at Chainarong restaurant. To mark the fiftieth anniversary of Chulalongkorn University, a rectangular-shaped building with a corrugated façade was built on a plot of land located on Phaya Thai Road. The design for the building emphasises the contrasts between solid and void and depth and lightness. A solid wall adds privacy to the building and separates it from the outside, while a void is used to provide natural light and cross-ventilation. The corrugated panels give the building texture and depth. In terms of facilities, it consists of a seminar room, a dormitory, an indoor court, a meeting room and a library.

≈ Pharotracha House 076 B

Location Chulalongkorn University, Phaya Thai Road, Pathum Wan
Architect/designer Unknown
Owner Chulalongkorn University
Construction period 1917–1929
Conservation award 1997

Pharotracha House is a two-storey building in a colonial style with a tower and elevated ground floor. The roof is gable on hip, decorated with fretwork on the eaves and balustrades. During the reign of King Rama VI, when this edifice was built, it was a residence of university administrators, foreign lecturers and officials. Later, it consecutively housed several university departments until the building became severely deteriorated. The university then decided to conserve it as a commemoration to Phraya Pharotracha (Mom Luang Thosthis Isarasena), the Commander of Chulalongkorn University from 1929 to 1952, who used to reside at this building. The edifice is conserved as evidence of residential buildings in those days and is used for the studies of Thai culture.

≈ Maha Chulalongkorn Building (Faculty of Arts Building) 077 B

Location Phaya Thai Road, Pathum Wan
Architect/designer Edward Healey
Owner Chulalongkorn University
Construction period 1914
Conservation award 1987

Maha Chulalongkorn Building, or the Faculty of Arts building, was initially built as a command building for the Civil Servants School which was founded in King Rama V's reign. On 26 March 1916, King Rama VI had the Civil Servants School established as Chulalongkorn University, the first university in Thailand. The building was used as the university administrative building and has consecutively housed a few faculties right up to the current one, the Faculty of Arts. In 1961, the Faculty of Arts was restructured and separated into six divisions: Thai, Eastern Languages, English, Western Languages, Geography and History and Library Science. Following a major restoration by the Fine Arts Department during the year 1996, the building is no longer used for academic functions, but rather only serves as a venue for ceremonial activities. The structure of the building consists of a three-tiered roof made of reinforced concrete with three porches. Its overall appearance is strong and dignified, with colonnades on the ground floor and verandas on the first.

≈ Chulalongkorn University Auditorium 078 B

Location Chulalongkorn University, Phaya Thai Road, Pathum Wan
Architect/designer Phra Phromphichit (U Laphanont) and Phra Sarotrattananimman
Owner/proprietor Chulalongkorn University
Construction period 1938–1939
Conservation award 2002

Chulalongkorn University Conference Hall is a building of applied Thai style which was designed to conform with the new construction techniques of those days – that is to say, it is a structure made of reinforced concrete. The commanding design was influenced by the *ubosatha* at Wat Rachathiwat which was designed by Prince Krommaphraya Narisaranuwattiwong. The project for the conference hall was initiated by the University President, Colonel Luang Phibunsongkhram. This was because Chulalongkorn University had an increasing number of students and more activities were therefore due to be held, but the school did not have a conference hall to house such activities. When the committee passed the issue, the design was carried out by Phra Phromphichit (U Laphanont) and Phra Sarotrattananimman, architects of the Fine Arts Department. Construction began in the year 1938 and was completed on 31 January 1939. Later, in 1963, the two wings were added on both sides, as can be seen today.

≈ Queen Saovabha Memorial Institute 079 B

Location 1871 Rama IV Road, Khwaeng Lumphini, Pathum Wan
Proprietor The Thai Red Cross Society
Construction period 1920–1922
Conservation award 1987

Queen Saovabha Memorial Institute was founded on 24 May 1920 by order of King Rama VI to commemorate the late Queen Si Patcharinthra. The neo-classical building has a hipped roof. One distinguished feature is the entrance which comprises a large round arch flanked by two towers with rusticated walls, inspired by the Roman triumphal arch. At first, it served as a new office for the Pastuer Institute which became the Thai Red Cross Society. The institute specialises in production of vaccines and vaccinations. There is also a snake farm in the compound which breeds poisonous snakes for vaccine preparations. This was founded in 1923 by Dr Leopold Robert, the first director. It is the world's second-oldest snake farm, the oldest being in Brazil.

» Lumpini Park Public Library 080 B

Location Ratchadamri Road, Lumpini
Owner Bangkok Metropolitan Administration
Construction period 1955
Conservation award 2007

The Lumpini Park Public Library was constructed in 1955 and opened for the first time on 24 June 1956. The library is situated to the rear of the King Rama VI Monument. It is a single-storey, reinforced concrete structure with a hipped roof which is accentuated by a gable in the middle. Upon it are written the words in stucco: Public Library of Bangkok, 2498 B.E. The edifice was built in a modern style with influences of classic and Thai architecture as seen in the capitals. In 1991, the building was extended as a

T-shaped building with an underground floor. The total area comprises 168 m².

≽ The Royal Bangkok Sports Club Polo Club 081 B

Location 18 Soi Polo, Wireless Road, Lumpinee
Architect/designer Moblex CO., Ltd.
Owner The Royal Bangkok Sports Club
Construction period 1981
Architectural design award 1984

In 1890, Franklin Hurst applied to Prince Devavongse Varopakorn, the Foreign Minister of Thailand, for permission to establish a race track and sports field. The purpose was to improve the standard of horse breeding and various other field sports. Therefore, the location of the club was to be in the heart of the city and easy to access. Royal approval was hereby graciously given, subject to the condition that membership of the club was not be confined to foreigners but also to include Thai people as well. Upon approval for its establishment by King Rama V, the club was officially opened in 1901. It is planned horizontally with a group of single-storey and two-storey buildings whose indoor spaces are designed to relate to the outdoor ones. Each function is placed proportionally and linked by covered walkways. The exterior walls have an exposed brick appearance, while the gable roofs are provided with overhangs, making the buildings look tall and slender; the aim here was to create an oriental atmosphere. The buildings are surrounded by sports fields for shade. Facilities include a clubhouse, a squash room, a badminton court, a tennis court, a swimming pool, a billiard room, a chess room, fitness facilities and a horse track.

4

American Ambassador's Residence 082 B

Location Wireless Road
Architect Horatio Victor Baily
Owner/proprietor American Embassy
Construction period 1914
Conservation award 1984

The American Embassy is a colonial-style building with a wooden structure and elevated floor. The front reception room is a large hall surrounded by windows opening on to the front lawn. The rooms have high ceilings decorated with fretwork above the windows.The house was originally a residence of Horatio Victor Baily, an English engineer. Later, during the Second World War, it was occupied by Japanese troops, before falling into a state of delapidation. In 1946, Edwin F. Stanton, the American Ambassador, and his wife – the first residents after the war – carried out a substantial restoration of the house until it was reinstated to its charming appearance as seen today.

» Dutch Ambassador's Residence 083 B

Location 106 Witthayu Road
Owner/proprietor Dutch Embassy
Construction period ca. 1895–1900
Conservation award 1987

The Dutch Embassy residence is a two-storey colonial house with a gable roof and a three-storey tower. Distinguished features are the double-roof of the tower and the decorative gable corners made of woodcarvings. The first owner of the house was Alphonse Poix, a French doctor who was a royal physician to King Rama V. When Dr Poix moved out in 1913, Prince Boworadet took up his place until 1933 before fleeing abroad for political reasons. However, the house was still his family's possession. It has been used as a residence for both Roman Catholic priests and the British Alumni Association, as well as being occupied by members of the British armed forces at the end of the Second World War. In 1948, the Dutch Government bought the house to be used as a residence for the ambassador. The first permanent Dutch Embassy was thus established in Thailand, since there had only been a consulate in former times.

« Nai Lert House 084 B

Location 4 Soi Somkid, Phloenchit Road
Architect Phraya Phakdinoraset
Owner Phuying Loesak Sombatsiri
Construction period 1905
Conservation award 1982

Phraya Phakdinoraset (Lert Setthabut), generally known as "Nai Lert", was arguably one of the greatest businessmen in the King Rama V period. In 1905, Nai Lert had his residence built on his estate, Park Nai Lert. He designed the house by himself, which resulted in a large, single-storey structure with an elevated floor built entirely of teak. It comprises a small house at the front connected to the large one at the rear. The house is suitable for a tropical climate in that it is airy, shady and well-ventilated – with notably tiered roofs which were probably inspired by Burmese architecture. Nai Lert lived and received guests at his house, while the park was open to the public on weekends and, occasionally, for Scout camping, before he passed away in 1945. Later, part of the house was renovated and some of the land divided to build a hotel.

≽ Spa 1930 (Doll House) 085 B

Location 42 Soi Ton Son, Phloenchit Road
Architects Mom Chao Wothayakon Worawan, Mom Ratchawong Chanwut Worawan
Owner Mom Chitra Worawan Na Ayutthaya
Construction period 1930–1931
Conservation award 1994

Spa 1930 was originally a residence of Professor Mom Chao Wothayakon Worawan, a distinguished architect who designed it as his own home, which in turn became his family home. The retro architecture is influenced by the British Arts and Crafts movement. It is a two-storey half-timber structure with an underground floor and framework made of sal and teak wood, filling the space with horizontally lined battens and finished with plaster. The specially designed rectangular roof tiles are made of a sand and cement mixture. The tiles at the rim were made to curve downward in order to cover the fascia, preventing rainwater penetration. At present, it has been converted into a luxury spa boasting a rustic atmosphere and top-class facilities.

Siam Commercial Bank Plc., Thanon Petchaburi Branch 086 B

Location 13 Petchaburi Road, Phaya Thai
Architect *Unknown*
Owner Siam Commercial Bank Plc.
Construction period 1929–1931
Conservation award 1982

The Thanon Petchaburi branch of the Siam Commercial Bank Plc. was originally the residence of Maha Ammat Tho Phraya Mahintharadechanuwat (Yai Sayamanont), the Governor of Monthol Nakhon Sawan. The house was built between 1929 and 1931, during the reign of King Rama VII. It is a two-storey, hipped-roof building with two porches on the front façade which are intentionally made to look different with the addition of a balustrade around one of the porch's hipped gable roofs. The style is distinctly unlike the classical buildings of former periods. After Phraya Mahintharadechanuwat passed away in the year 1950, the Siam Commercial Bank bought the house from his heir to use as their branch office in 1971. Later, in 1995, a new office building was built behind the house. A major restoration was then carried out, by which altered elements were restored and the interior renovated to suit the style of the building. At present, the building is used as a conference hall and is a well-recognised landmark.

Suan Phakkad Palace 087 B

Location 352–354 Si Ayutthaya Rd, Ratchathewi
Owner Chumbhot-Pantip Foundation
Construction period 1952
Conservation award 1994

Wang Suan Phakkad, a group of traditional Thai houses in the heart of Bangkok, comprises eight Thai houses and the Lacquer Pavilion (Ho Khian). The houses are mostly of a central Thai style, while only one house is of a northern style. The Lacquer Pavilion is built in the style of Buddhist scripture halls at Ayutthaya. The exterior walls are carved wood panels and the interior walls are decorated with Lai Rod Nam (washed gilded lacquer). The three buildings at

the front date back to over a century ago. These were originally located near Wat Phichaiyat in Bangkok, but were transported a few times until 1952, when Major General Prince Chumbhot Phongboriphatr Krommamuen Nakhon Sawan Sakdiphinit had them relocated to Suan Phakkad. Buildings in the compound have been adapted to serve their new function as a museum for the collection of ancient art artefacts which belonged to the Prince and Mom Ratchawong Pantip Boripat, his wife. These are now in the care of the Chumbhot-Pantip Foundation.

Makkasan Train Warehouse is an example of a modern architecture with running-bond brick masonry, a reinforced concrete structure, a trussed roof and segmental arched windows. Its overall appearance can be described as simple yet remarkable. The warehouse underwent a major restoration in 1951 after being damaged by the war. It is currently one of the largest train repair and maintenance centres of the State Railway of Thailand.

≈ Makkasan Train Warehouse 088 B

Location Nikhom Makkasan Road, Makkasan, Ratchathewi
Owner State Railway of Thailand
Construction period 1907–1910
Conservation award 2006

During the reign of King Rama V, when the Royal Railway Department was founded, the department under the Ministry of Public Works was divided into two separate ones: namely, the Northern Line Railway Department and the Southern Line Railway Department. These were subsequently merged in 1917 under the authority of His Royal Highness Krommaphra Kamphaengphet Akharayothin, the Commander of the Royal Railway Department. Their warehouses were also combined and have since been located at Makkasan.

» Xavier Church 089 B

Location Victory Monument
Architect Casa Co., Ltd.
Proprietor Xavier Hall Jesuit Fathers
Construction period 1972
Architectural design award 1984

Since there are a lot of worshippers who regularly attend the services, the layout of the chapel had to be visible from the main entrance and the design needed to suit the Catholic Church's activities. Therefore, the Father's residences are linked with the chapel. The exterior and interior atmosphere of the building is characterised by traditional Thai architecture. The building conveys the idea that God is at the centre of one's heart by providing a skylight to let the sun shine through the building, illuminating the

cross and allowing its golden hues to stand out. The altar's panels are decorated with traditional Thai paintings, while the fish scales on the curved roof depict a traditional Thai temple. The chapel uses sliding louvred doors to allow air circulation through the building. There is a terrace around the chapel for convenience purposes, especially for religious ceremonies when worshippers come together for services.

» Phaya Thai Palace 090 B

Location Nikhom Makkasan Road, Makkasan, Ratchathewi
Architect/designer Unknown
Owner State Railway of Thailand
Construction period 1907–1910
Conservation award 2006

Phaya Thai Palace was initially built by King Rama V as his countryside resort during his visits to the royal paddy fields in the Phaya Thai district. Buildings from that period were typically small and simple. The halls are an example of romantic architecture and are decorated with stucco and woodcarvings. Several of them have a high domed roof. The interiors are decorated with frescos and stucco. Overall, the palace is picturesque, extraordinary and elaborate in appearance, with fine craftsmanship. The compound also boasts a historic landscape, namely the scenic Roman Garden which is also in the romantic style. Following the reign of King Rama VI, the palace was rehabilitated as a hotel called Hotel Phaya Thai. It was followed by the first Thai government broadcasting station and the Pramongkutklao Medicine Centre. Today, it is known as Pramongkutklao Hospital. The halls have been renovated to serve the hospital's multiple needs.

Round Building, Mahidol University

091 B

Location 272 Rama VI Rd, Ratchathewi
Architect/designer Amon Sriwong
Owner/proprietor Mahidol University
Construction period 1965
Conservation award 2010

Round Building (Tuek Klom) denotes a futuristic spaceship-like building which serves as a lecture hall. The building is called Tuek Klom because, when looking at it from above, it has a circular form. The purpose of this was to enhance visual communication and articulate sound spaces.

As a result, walls in the rooms are joined at obtuse angles with the one focal point being the podium. The ground floor has an open space for student activities and skylights on the roof to provide natural light. Wooden panels were pressed into the concrete, creating a dripping texture on the outer ceiling. Stone veneer is applied on the exterior stucco finish at the base of the building, while the roof is decorated with ceramic tiles. The building comprises four 250-seat lecture rooms and one 500-seat lecture room. The largest room is used for ceremonies as well.

Thai Military Bank, Sanampao Branch 092 B

Location 300/1 Phaholyothin Road, Samsennai, Phaya Thai
Architect/designer Design 103 Limited
Owner Thai Military Bank Co., Ltd.
Construction period 1975
Architectural design award 1982

The Sanampao branch of the Thai Military Bank is a single-storey building. The front façade is oriented towards the south and includes a towering sign which is visible from a distance, denoting the name of the bank and a side street for the convenience of customers. The building is set back from the street and pavement by a lawn and plaza – features intended to draw people into an inviting environment with a pedestrian access. In the event of rain, a waiting area is provided at the entrance. To ensure customer safety, the interior of the building cannot be seen from the outside.

Mekhala Ruchi Pavilion 093 B

Location Ratchawithi Road, Phaya Thai
Architect/designer Mario Tamagno
Owner Pramongkutklao Medicine Centre, Royal Thai Army Medical Department
Construction period 1919–1920
Conservation award 1997

The Mekhala Ruchi Pavilion is a small building that was originally named Phra Tamnak Udomwanaphon. It is part of the Phaya Thai Palace. Following its construction, King Rama VI commissioned new halls and pavilions to be built, including Phra Tamnak Udomwanaphon, a modest edifice used as the King's study. The new halls were completed in 1922. The two-storey pavilion is made of teakwood, although columns, beams, and foundations are made of ferroconcrete. Terracotta tiles were used for the roof. The plan of this structure comprises several rectangular and oval shapes, resulting in a composition of roofs, which includes hip, lean-to, and dome roofs; these three types are integrated into an exquisite romantic architecture. The pavilion is beautifully adorned with stained glass. A major restoration was carried out in 1994. The pavilion came to be used by the King's barber.

≈ Portuguese Ambassador's Residence 094 B

Location Soi Captain Bush, Charoen Krung Road
Owner/proprietor Portuguese Embassy
Construction period 1860
Conservation award 1984

The Portuguese Ambassador's residence is a two-storey colonial-style building with a hipped roof and gabled front porch – an indication of neo-Palladian influences. The front gable is decorated with the emblem of Portugal. The entrance on the ground floor and the window frames comprise three connecting round arches alternating with superimposed pilasters. The grand hall is located on the ground floor, while the upper floor is flanked with verandas along the front and rear. The entrance is decorated with blue and white ceramic tiles from Portugal. Following the second defeat of Ayutthaya to Burma, the Portuguese were the first Western nation to renew contact with Siam. Later, King Rama IV wrote an official letter to the Queen of Portugal inviting her country to establish a permanent consulate in Thailand. The Portuguese government thus sent a group of builders with materials such as stone, glass, and furniture from Gua, India, and construction began in 1860. This house has continued to be used as the Portuguese Ambassador's residence until the present day.

» O.P. Place 095 B

Location 30/1 Charoen Krung Rd 38,
Architect/designer Unknown
Owner/proprietor Surathip Co., Ltd.
Construction period 1908
Conservation award 1982

O.P. Place is a shopping centre in an ancient commercial building dating back to 1908, during the late period of King Rama V's reign. Originally, the building was built as the Falck & Beidek Store. It then housed Oriental Plaza Shopping Centre, followed by O.P. Place. The present owner is Surathip Co., Ltd. The two-storey building is designed in a neoclassical style and has a rectangular plan. There is a three-storey tower at each wing. The edifice is decorated with mouldings, superimposed pilasters, rusticated walls and arched windows. Distinguished features include the three gabled porches and an antique stone elephant. Since being established in the previous century, the building has proudly and successfully retained its original features as well as its function as a shopping centre.

The Ashwood Gallery
3rd Floor
O.P. PLACE

≈ The China House, Mandarin Oriental Hotel 096 B

Location Charoen Krung Road 38
Owner Mandarin Oriental Hotel
Construction period ca. 1923
Conservation award 1994

The China House, originally called Pagoda Building, is designed in a Victorian gingerbread style. It constitutes a two-storey brick masonry building with a hipped roof and an open court in the centre featuring arched openings and fretwork ornamentation. The building was originally built as a residence. It has currently been renovated to house a Chinese restaurant operated by the Mandarin Oriental Hotel. The interior is beautifully decorated with Chinese art. The Mandarin Oriental Hotel has rented this house from the Crown Property Bureau.

≥ Mandarin Oriental Hotel 097 B

Location 48 Trok Oriental, Charoen Krung Road
Architect/designer Stefano Cardu
Owner The Oriental Hotel (Thailand) Plc.
Construction period 1885
Conservation award 2002

The Mandarin Oriental Hotel – which ranks number one in Thailand and one of the best in the world – was founded circa 1870. The two-storey Author's Wing, the hotel's historic building, is an example of a neoclassical architecture. It features a symmetrical plan with a central porch accentuated by a fractable. This is embellished with stucco depicting a rising sun, with the name of the hotel written below. The arched windows are decorated with wooden fretwork, while the interior is furnished with oriental furniture. These features are all integrated into an atmosphere of a wealthy family home from the olden days that feels splendid and welcoming at the same time. This is despite the fact that the Mandarin Oriental Hotel has had its ups and downs throughout the past century, involving changes of ownership and renovations. The hotel used to receive many of the world's most distinguished personalities, as well as being used as a headquarters for Japanese troops during the Second World War. Nevertheless, the Authors' Wing still stands today, ready to infuse guests with a sense of nostalgia.

Study Hall, Assumption Convent School

098 B

Location 25 Charoen Krung 40
Architect/designer Unknown
Owner/proprietor Assumption Convent School
Construction period 1904–1905
Conservation award 2007

Assumption Convent School is the first school to be managed by the Sisters of St. Paul de Chartres of Thailand during the reign of King Rama V, in 1904. The three-storey study hall of the Assumption Convent School was officially opened in 1905. The architecture is colonial in style with visible classical influences, including a hipped roof with a projecting gable portico. The building is composed of arched windows whose wooden panels are fitted with louvre awning inner panels, while the lower parts of the windows comprise stucco balustrades. The classrooms are enclosed with a network of corridors. Floors and ceilings are wooden, while the upper part of the door panels are wooden louvres and above the doors are wooden openwork fanlights. The building projects a strong, stately and simple appearance. It is well ventilated and suitable for the climate of the particular area – a distinctive characteristic of colonial architecture. The study hall has been continuously used and is well conserved to this day. The gleaming white façades give the building a clean appearance.

099 B

การศึกษา
คือ
แสงสว่างของชีวิต

« Assumption Cathedral 099 B

Location Soi Oriental, Charoen Krung Road 40
Architect/designer Unknown
Owner Bangkok Roman Catholic Mission
Construction period 1909
Conservation award 1994

Assumption Cathedral was founded circa 1809. Later, in 1909, a new church was built to serve the increasing number of Christians within the community. The church was designed by a French architect with a wall-bearing structure and a raft foundation made of logs tied together. The height at the top of the towers is 32 m and 25.6 m at the top of the gable, while the plan is rectangular and laid out on an east-west axis. The architecture is gothic revival in style, whereas the interior is decorated with classic elements. During the Second World War, the church was partially damaged; a restoration with structural consolidation was thus carried out. The tension rods which hold the longitudinal walls together today were fitted. Inside, the church has a round arched ceiling in a Romanesque style which is decorated with stars and supported by colonnades. The walls are adorned with frescos and stucco. The interior space is divided into three parts: the altar, the seating area and the entrance hall – above which is a mezzanine where the choirs and a large organ once stood.

¥ French Ambassador's Residence 100 B

Location Soi Rong Phasi, Charoen Krung Road
Owner/proprietor French Embassy
Construction period King Rama IV period
Conservation award 1984

The three-storey French Ambassador's residence is a colonial-style edifice situated on the banks of the Chao Phraya River. It has a two-storey front porch and two outdoor staircases on both sides. On the pediment is written the monogram FR, which stands for France. Wooden fretwork and woodcarvings in a simple design are examples of its ornamentation, while each floor is surrounded by verandas. The overall atmosphere conveyed is that of cosiness and friendliness. Originally, the house served as both the embassy office and residence, but since the office moved to a new building it has only functioned as the residence of the ambassador. A major restoration was undertaken from 1959 to 1968, which was followed by an interior renovation to give the house a more modern look.

East Asiatic Co., Ltd. 101 B

Location Oriental Alley, Bang Rak
Architect Annibale Rigotti
Owner/proprietor Oriental Hotel
Construction period ca. 1900
Conservation award 1984

The office of the East Asiatic Co., Ltd. is a three-storey brick masonry building with a hipped roof and a wall-bearing structure. It is a classic example of renaissance revival architecture, featuring prominent round arches and a porch accentuated by a front panel of brick masonry which is built to match the height of the roof. The building is set back from the river, boasting scenic views across the waterfront. It is the towering entrance with its broad palatial staircase that makes the building distinguishable and stately in appearance. The company was founded in 1884 by Captain Hans Niels Andersen, a Danish mariner who came to Thailand via the Chao Phraya River and anchored at Oriental Pier. This building was used as an office until 1995, when it was relocated to Lumphini Tower. The old office building, however, has been conserved as a historic building and was registered as a national monument in the year 2001.

≈ Wat Suan Phlu

102 B

Location 58 Charoen Krung Road
Architect/designer Unknown
Owner/proprietor Wat Suan Phlu
Construction period Prior to 1934
Conservation award 2002

Wat Suan Phlu was built circa 1797 on a plot of land which was formerly a betel leaf farm by the Chinese community. The Ordination Hall was built in 1798 and the Gathering Hall in 1934. The century-old monks' residences have still been well conserved. These are built in the same design, namely two-storey wooden structures decorated with fretwork on the sunshades and balustrades. The atmosphere is simple and peaceful, helped in part by the fact that the temple grounds are kept very clean, tidy and green, as appropriate to a religious place.

⊻ Local Bangkok Museum

103 B

Location 273 Charoen Krung Rd 43,
Owner/proprietor Bangkok Metropolis
Construction period 1937
Conservation award 2008

The Local Bangkok Museum in Bang Rak focuses on the way of life of the middle-class citizens of Bangkok before and after the Second World War, encompassing the period from 1937 to 1957. It consists of four individual buildings. The first building was built from wood in 1937 and has a hip roof. The atmosphere inside the house is still the same as the olden days owing to the preservation of the bedroom, living room and furniture. The second building houses an exhibition presenting daily life belongings that were used in the past, such as kitchenware and mechanical equipment. The former owner was an Indian doctor who graduated in England. Therefore, all belongings in the house express the differences between Eastern and Western culture. The third building has a ground-floor exhibition containing several documents – such as title deeds, family registrations and maps collected by the householder – while an exhibition on the second floor presents holistic images of Bangkok. As for the fourth building, this has been converted into a library offering a wide range of books.

Nielson Hays Library 104 B

Location 195 Surawong Road
Architect/designer Mario Tamagno, Giovanni Ferrero
Owner/proprietor Society of the Nielson Hays Library
Construction period 1921
Conservation award 1982

In 1869, a group of missionaries' wives who lived in Bangkok gathered to form a reading group called the Bangkok Ladies Bazaar Association. Later, Dr Hays built a library hall as a memorial for his beloved wife under the name Nielson Hays Library. The building boasts a neo-classical style and is symmetrically planned with a circular entrance crowned by a domed roof which leads to an H-shaped reading hall. It is so well integrated, so well designed and so elegant that the architect himself, Mario Tamagno, disclosed that it was his favourite work whose every detail he had attended to. The building has served as a library since its completion. Nevertheless, there have been some alterations: namely, the entrance hall has been converted into an art gallery.

≈ Silom Village Trade Centre 105 B

Location 286 Silom Road
Architect/designer Unknown
Owner Prapassorn Aksoramat
Construction period King Rama V period
Conservation award 2002

Silom Village Trade Centre is a shopping centre that has been rehabilitated to form a group of seventeen teakwood houses which were built during the late King Rama V period. The first owner was Siao Song Pae Sibunrueang. The houses were inherited within the family, right up to Prasongsak Aksoramat who perceived their value and subsequently had them converted into a shopping centre and tourist attraction. The project was thus opened on 29 November 1980 and now comprises restaurants, souvenir shops and arts and crafts shops. Since its opening, the site has become a famous place in Bangkok for its alfresco walkable spaces. Authentic Thai food and culture are easy to find in the entertainment venue.

↱ British Club 106 B

Location Surawong Road
Owner/proprietor British Club
Construction period 1910
Conservation award 2006

The British Club was founded in 1903 during the reign of King Rama V as a meeting place and entertainment centre for British expatriates in Thailand. When first established, the club comprised approximately sixty to seventy members, almost

all of them businessmen and merchants. The original two-storey clubhouse was designed in a colonial style and opened on 6 July 1903. In 1910, the old clubhouse was demolished and the new one built. It is believed to have been designed by a British architect whose name, however, remains unknown. The new clubhouse is a two-storey building in a Georgian style which was popularised in England by Sir Christopher Wren. It has a symmetrical layout with a central portico comprising arches and a temple-front design evoking Ancient Greece to give the building a stable, strong and dignified appearance. The building has been well maintained.

» Suriyasai House 107 **B**

Location Surawong Road, Si Phraya, Bangrak
Architect/designer Unknown
Owner Estate of Phit Bunnak
Construction period King Rama V period
Conservation award 2004

Baan Suriyasai is an amalgamation of the words *suriya* ("the sun" – the emblem of the Bunnak family) and *asai* ("to live"). It therefore translates as "living place of the Bunnak family". Baan Suriyasai is a two-storey half-brick half-wooden house. The architecture is an intriguing mixture of Victorian and colonial styles. It is said to have been designed by an Italian architect who was amongst those to have designed the Anatasamakhom throne hall. The first change to Baan Suriyasai occurred approximately forty years ago, when a new two-storey, L-shaped house was built at the front of the site on the corner where Surawong Road meets Sap Road. The new building was rented out to a French businessman and used as the first Citroën car showroom in Thailand. Later, Phit Bunnak had a small two-storey building built as a home for her daughter's newly-wed family. Baan Suriyasai has currently been developed into a small shopping complex with a furniture showroom and restaurants. The rooms on the upper floor have been renovated to house a museum of the Bunnak family.

Abdulrahim House 108 B

Location 960 Rama IV Road
Architect/designer Unknown
Owner Prachum Abdulrahim
Construction period ca. 1907–1908
Conservation award 1982

Abdulrahim House originally belonged to an Indian merchant whose father came to settle in Thailand during the reign of King Rama V. The house was built as a countryside resort so that he would not have to travel as far as Hua Hin for his holidays. Later, the house was rented to foreigners who worked in Bangkok for short periods of time. Because it was intended as a resort house, its design places emphasis on an airy atmosphere and good ventilation, something that is achieved through the application of wood and a high elevated floor featuring a wide roof deck. The gingerbread-style architecture is adorned with wooden fretwork on fascia boards and gable corners with star and crescent motifs (Islamic symbols) and floral designs. This is also in keeping with the Islamic rule prohibiting the depiction of human and animal forms for religious art and architecture.

St. Joseph Convent School, Chapel 109 B

Location 7 Convent Road, Silom
Architect/designer Alfredo Rigazzi
Owner St. Joseph Convent School
Construction period 1907
Conservation award 2007

The first school building had two storeys and was built of brick. It was said to have a basement for storing water and a foundation made of large logs. The school grounds were lush and green owing to the trees. Some parts of the land were allocated to the raising of pigs and turkeys.

In the year 1969, the 72-year Building was constructed, and, in 1987, the Trinity Conference Hall was built, dramatically changing the appearance of the edifice in comparison with its founding period. Nevertheless, among the new buildings there still exists the school chapel, a historic building which to this day functions as a venue for religious activities. The chapel is a three-storey rectangular brick building in a classic revival style. Architectural elements here aim to emphasise serenity and dignity. The chapel has a nave flanked by two-storey galleries and an apse in the form of a Palladian motif. The walls are fitted with wooden louvred windows to provide good ventilation. Approximately thirty years ago, some parts of the chapel were damaged by fire, including the ceilings which have now been repaired. The restoration attempted to preserve the original features of the building.

≽ Belgian Ambassador's Residence 110 B

Location Soi Phiphat, Silom Road
Architect/designer Mario Tamagno
Owner/proprietor Belgian Embassy
Construction period 1917
Conservation award 1997

The Belgian Ambassador's residence originally belonged to Nuam Thonawanik. It was later sold to a lawyer who worked as a government consultant. The house is art nouveau in style with a hipped gable roof: simple yet stately in appearance. In 1935, the Belgian government granted permission to establish a permanent embassy in Thailand; the property was thus bought and used as the Belgian Ambassador's residence. Ever since, it has received a number of VIP guests. Notable examples include King Baudouin and Queen Fabiola of Belgium.

» Plan Toys (Raklook Kindergarten) 111 B

Location 64/1 North Sathorn Road 10
Architect Plan Architect Co., Ltd.
Owner Plan Education Co., Ltd.
Construction period 1988
Architectural design award 1989

The design concept was inspired by the spatial layout of a gathering hall in a Thai Buddhist temple. Traditionally, a spacious pavilion functions as a classroom for novices and children, while an open unpaved area just beyond the roof is used as a playground or for outdoor assemblies. Such an arrangement of space offers a sense of freedom. A similar spatial composition has been applied to the new school to create a world of open spaces within a relatively small building. Each part of the building was designed to respond to the others, as well as to its surroundings, be they trees, roads, nearby constructions, climate, light and, of course, people. The physical limits of space are thereby minimised by their constant relationship to the outdoors. Children can move around freely and explore their surroundings to satisfy their curiosity. At present, the building functions as an office, a restaurant and a showroom which has a variety of children's books and toys.

» Plan House 112 B

Location 64 North Sathorn Road 10
Architect Plan Architecs Co., Ltd.
Owner/proprietor Plan Group
Construction period 1987
Architectural design award 1987

The design concept behind Plan House is twofold; it is designed to stand out from the surrounding buildings, but at the same time is to tastefully reflect and respect its environment. A landscaped external stairway serves each level, while a spiral staircase illuminated by glass blocks is a defining feature of the interior. The idiosyncratic style of the building is postmodern. The structure comprises offices, a library which is open to the public, a photo studio and a multi-purpose room.

St. Louis Grand Terrace Condominium 113 B

Location 15/200 South Sathorn Road 11
Architect Architects and Associates Co.
Owner Metro Star Property Company
Architectural design award 2008

The building façade consists of simple lines of either precast concrete or voids, alternating with the placement of transparent and frosted glass. The podium is decorated with a navy blue aluminium mesh in a criss-cross pattern created by askew and wavy lines. The tower area primarily adopts the form of the curved line of a sailboat. The design addresses the composition of the shape, emphasising the plane on both rears of the sailboat, covering the centre core on both sides. The plane is highlighted by void openings using horizontal strips of green glass on each floor, juxtaposed with the vertical composition caused by closely adjacent horizontal lines of stainless steel tubes. The building also features horizontal fins made of aluminium composite cladding above the glass voids. The plane on the front elevation is designed to be the mass of the balcony using precast rails and horizontal navy blue aluminium safety rails. The line descends along with the curve of the rear of the sailboat. Facilities at St. Louis Grand Terrace include twenty-four-hour security, a sauna, a gym and a swimming pool.

Blue Elephant Restaurant (Thai Chinese Chamber of Commerce) 114 B

Location 233 South Sathorn Road, Yan Nawa
Owner/proprietor Blue Elephant Restaurant (rented from the Thai Chinese Chamber of Commerce)
Construction period 1915
Conservation award 2001

Blue Elephant Restaurant (Thai Chinese Chamber of Commerce) is a three-storey building in a renaissance revival style with discernible Chinese architectural influences. Notable features include the fractable – which draws comparisons to the Dutch bell-shaped gable – and arched windows elaborately decorated with mouldings. The upper floor windows are sheltered with hipped roofs which were added during a later period. The building was originally an office of the Bombay Burma Trading Company. Later, during the reign of King Rama VII, the Association of Chinese Commerce in Thailand (the present Thai Chinese Chamber of Commerce) bought the house and land to be used as their new office. The official opening ceremony was held on 14 January 1930, presided over by King Rama VII and Queen Rambhaibhanni. At present, The Thai Chinese Chamber of Commerce has now moved to a new building at the back of the compound and the old office premises have subsequently been rented to the Blue Elephant Restaurant which serves the finest Thai cuisine.

⌃ Baan Pra Nond Bed & Breakfast 115 B

Location 18/1 Charoen Rat Road, Yannawa
Architect/designer Unknown
Owner/proprietor Tasma Cotsmire
Construction period Unknown
Conservation award 2010

The two-storey Baan Pra Nond Bed & Breakfast is a classic example of Thai colonial architecture. It was a former residence of Khun Pra Nonthapanya Makaranond who, owing to reasons linked to his work and expanding family, decided to move out and rent the house. It was then left unoccupied for more than fifteen years until the property was eventually inherited by his granddaughter, who renovated it and turned it into a guesthouse called Baan Pra Nond. The owner maintains the home-like atmosphere of the old house as much as possible by mixing contemporary furniture with vintage examples – that is to say, items which have been used in the house for more than seventy years. The structure of the new building is also the same as the existing one. Altogether, the guesthouse provides a friendly atmosphere and takes pains to ensure that visitors feel right at home amidst their surroundings.

↱ M. R. Kukrit Heritage Home 116 B

Location 19 Soi Phra Phinit, South Sathorn Road
Architect Mom Ratchawong Kukrit Pramoj
Owner Mom Luang Rongrit Pramoj
Construction period 1960
Conservation award 2001

M. R. Kukrit Heritage Home, which is generally known as Ban Soi Suan Phlu, comprises a group of traditional Thai teakwood stilt houses which M. R. Kukrit Pramoj bought from different places to be grouped on his plot of land. M. R. Kukrit Pramoj was the thirteenth Prime Minister of Thailand and National Artist of Thailand for Literature. This prominent scholar was educated at Oxford. The house contains Ruean Khon, a large pavilion used as a reception and multi-purpose hall which was built ten years after he moved into the house. Next to Ruean Khon is a fountain court in front of the group of three houses, whose names are Ruean Khun Ya, Ruean Non and Ruean Nangsue. In addition there is Ho Phra, Ho Khwang and Ho Nok. The house is open to visitors, while all entrance fees go towards the Kukrit 80 Foundation under the Royal Patronage of Her Royal Highness Princess Maha Chakri Sirindhorn.

≽ Baan No. 139 Soi Thian Siang 117 B

Location 139 Soi Thian Siang, South Sathorn Road
Owner Kasem Chatikawanit
Construction period 1910
Conservation award 1982

Kasem Chatikawanit's house is entirely built of teak in an architectural style referred to as the Black and White House. This denotes a vernacular design integrated with English half-timber, including a black framework and white walls. The building contains a gabled hip roof and wooden louvred windows. It is decidedly simple in its overall appearance. Khun Phra Loha (Phraya Phitsanusaen) had his house built circa 1910 from teak he bought wholesale from the Bombay Burma Trading Company. Later he sold the house to Phraya Athikonprakat, Kasem's father, who ordered a balcony to be added to the house. The original roof tiles were made of cement, but have since been changed to asbestos during repairs which were carried out in 1990.

Urbana Sathorn 118 B

Location 55 South Sathorn Road, Tung Maha Mek, Sathorn
Architects Architects 49 Limited
Owner Urbana Estate Co., Ltd.
Construction period 2006
Architectural design award 2008

The Urbana Sathorn comprises apartments and serviced apartments. The design is optimised for maximum efficiency with a total of thirty-six floors accommodating 208 apartment units. Sixty-three units are serviced apartments located between the eighth and fourteenth floors, while a further 145 apartments are located between the fifteenth and thirty-sixth storeys. Public space provided includes the lobby, restaurants, tennis courts, a small basketball court, a sauna, an aerobics room, squash courts, badminton courts, a fitness room, a large lap pool with a jacuzzi, a playground, retail spaces, a commerce centre and a laundromat. The Urbana Sathorn is a high-rise building designed to best suit a contemporary urban lifestyle. The 14 m curtain wall in the lobby area affords maximum views across the cityscape. The building's materials are a combination of modern and natural ones – for example timber used for the louvres. Not only do these give unique look to the building, but they also reflect the tropical climate of Bangkok.

Esmeralda 119 B

Location Soi Ngamduplee, South Sathorn Road, Tung Maha Mek
Architect/designer Design & Develop
Construction period 1975
Architectural design award 1982

Esmeralda is a high-income residence. Each unit is designed to have separated walls and a layout scheme tailored to provide occupants with the utmost privacy. The building is divided into two separate structures with a glistening swimming pool and spacious courtyard in the middle to bring them harmoniously together. The apartments boast a total of sixty-two units; each unit comprises a living room, a dining room, two to three bedrooms, two bathrooms, a kitchen, a servant's room and a washing area featuring ceramic and parquet floors throughout. On the eleventh and twelfth floors there can be found luxury rooms – the most expensive in the building – which are noticeably larger with internal apartment stairs. The building also contains a trash disposal facility as well as a laundry area. The towering white edifice is made of reinforced concrete and has a post-and-beam structure.

Between the City and its Airports

DUSIT
PHAYA THAI
RATCHATHEWI
POM PRAP SATTRU PHAI
PATHUM WAN
BANG RAK
SATHON
Nakhon Chai Si Road
Ratchasima Nuea Road
Sukhothai Road
Phichai
Rat Withi Road
Amphon Garden
Bangkok Zoo
Rama V Road
Sret Siri Road
Thoet Damri Road
Si Rat Expressway
Rama VI Road
Soi Ari Samphan
Ari
Phahon Yothin Road
Soi Phahon Yothin 2
Sanam Pao
Chitlada Place Park
Ratchawithi Road
Si Rat
Expressway
Soi Ratchawithi
Don Mueang
Din Da
Si Ayutthaya Road
Sawankhalok Road
Yothi Road
Victory Monument
Phitsanulok Road
Krung Kasem Road
Rang Nam Road
Phayathai Road
Ratchaprarop Road
Chaloem Maha Nakhon Expressway
Lan Luang Road
Phaya Thai
Ratchaprarop
Maha Nak
Phet Buri Road
Rama VI Road (Below Expressway)
Banthat Thong Road
Ratchathewi
Bamrung Muang Road
Rama I Road
National Stadium
Siam
Chit Lom
Phloen Chit Road
Phloen Chit
Ratchadamri Road
Witthayu Road
Soi Chulalongkorn 12
Krung Kasem Road
Wong Wian 22 July
Hua Lamphon Railway Station
Charu Muang Road (Below Expressway)
Banthat Thong
Soi Chulalongkorn 9
Soi Lang Suan
Soi Ruam Ruedi
Henri Dunant Road
Ratchadamri
Charoen Krung Road
Hua Lamphong
Rama IV Road
Sarasin Road
Suan Lumphini Lake
Lumphini Park
Chao Phraya River
Si Phraya Road
Sam Yan
Si Lom
Sala Daeng
Lumphini
Surawong Road
Silom Road
Chong Nonsi
Sathon Tai Road
Sathon Nuea Road
Surasak Road
Surasak
Saphan Taksin
Soi Suan Phlu
Naradhiwas Rajanagarindra Road
Nang Lynchee Road
Yen Akat Road
0
1 km
N5
N4
N3
N2
N1
W1
CEN
E1
E2
S1
S2
S3
S5
S6
M

Don Mueang Tollway
Soi Pracha Suk
Ratchadaphisek Road
Ratchadaphisek 18
Huai Khwang
HUAI KHWANG
Pracha Songkhro Road
DIN DAENG
Soi Pracha Uthit 19
Pracha Uthit Road
Lat Phrao
Thailand Cultural Centre
Watthanatham Road
Thiam Ruam Mit Road
Samsen
Pracha Songkhro 2
Chuat Yai
Phra Ram 9
Asok Din Daeng Road
Rama IX Road
Samsen Nai
Si Rat Expressway
Royal City Avenue
Phetchaburi
Saen Saep
Phet Buri Road
Soi Sukhumvit 13
Soi Sukhumvit 21
Sukhumvit Road
Asok
Sukhumvit
Soi Sukhumvit 49
Soi Sukhumvit 55
Soi Sukhumvit 63
Ekkamai Soi 22
Soi Sukhumvit 39
WATTHANA
Soi Sukhumvit 16
Ratchadaphisek Road
Soi Sukhumvit 22
Phrom Phong
Ekkamai Soi 5
Lake Ratchada
Soi Sukhumvit 24
Soi Sukhumvit 26
Thong Lo
Queen Sirikit National Conv. Centre
KHLONG TOEI
Soi Sukhumvit 36
Ban Kluai Tai Alley
Ekkamai
Rama IV Road
Thang Rot Fai Sai Kao Road
Sunthon Kosa Road
Chaloem Maha Nakhon Expressway
Phra Khanong
120 121 122 123 124 125 126 127 128 129 130 131 132 133 134 135 136 137 138
E4 E5 E6 E7 E8

5

FORTUNER
DEESTONE

« Doi Chaang Signature 120 B

Location 46 Soi Prasanmit, Watthana
Architect/designer Design 103 Limited
Owner Piya International Co., Ltd.
Construction period 1981
Architectural design award 1982

Doi Chaang Signature is a group of two- to three-storey buildings in a Bavarian architectural style with a central courtyard, such as can be found in a typical suburban village in this area of Germany. The design of the central courtyard seeks to convey the atmosphere of a small road in the village decorated with small cottages and vintage wooden posts to inject it with more life and ease off the contradiction between its neighbouring buildings and surroundings. The building is a wood-frame structure with reinforced concrete. The exterior consists of masonry walls coated with rough plaster – i.e. the same texture as many buildings found in Bavaria. The texture of the interior walls is notably different in each room, depending on their use.

≽ Prasanmit Building Srinakharinwirot University 121 B

Location Soi Sukhumvit 23, Watthana
Architect Phian Sombatpiam
Owner Srinakharinwirot University
Construction period 1950
Conservation award 2007

Prasanmit Building was designed to serve as the first lecture building of the Higher Teachers' Training School. It is made of reinforced concrete with a three-storey central core flanked by two-storey wings. The central core is 19 m wide, each wing is 10 m wide, while the total area is 1,233 m^2. The building features hipped roofs over the wings and a gabled central core finished with asbestos tiles. Overall, the building is an example of modern architecture owing to its dignified simplicity. Decorative elements include cast cement balustrades in a geometric design. Terrazzo flooring is used for the corridors, while the floors of the rooms are paved with wooden planks. Prasanmit Building is curently being used as Srinakharinwirot University Archives, Culture and Art Institution.

≈ Siam Society 122 B

Location 131 Sukhumwit 21 Road
Architect/designer Edward Healey
Owner Siam Society
Construction period 1932
Conservation award 2001

The Siam Society under Royal Patronage was established in 1904, towards the end of King Rama V's reign. The objective of the society is to encourage the study and promotion of arts and sciences concerning Thailand and neighbouring countries. It has been under Royal Patronage of each successive King since its foundation. The architecture is Western with some Thai characteristics. The building functions as a conference hall, library and office. An Ethnological Museum has also been set up in the compound which comprises the Kalae-style Khamthieng House from northern Thailand and a house from Suphanburi in Central Thailand called Saeng Arun House, where exhibitions on local ways of life and local tools are held.

» Indian Embassy 123 B

Location 46 Soi Prasanmit (Sukhumvit 23), Watthana
Architect/designer Moblex Co., Ltd.
Owner/proprietor Indian Embassy
Construction period 1979
Architectural design award 1982

The Indian Embassy is a double-storey building with a mezzanine. The design for the mezzanine wall is adorned with modern Indian art which can be seen from

the hallway and the waiting area. At the front of the building are Indian-style ivory and metal sculptures and, to the left, is the service area. The hallway is connected with the consulate area through the reception and the visa services. It is also linked with the courtyard, where outdoor parties are sometimes held. The selection of structure and materials is well balanced across the building. Decorative interior elements include round posts and terrazzo flooring on the ground floor. As for the exterior and the terrace, the floors are adorned with red clay tiles which continue through to the base of the curved wall in order to bring the designs for the terrace and the building together. Above the wall is a sunshade crafted in unique curved lines.

Mini Showroom 124 B

Location 131 Sukhumwit 21 Road
Architect/designer Edward Healey
Proprietor Siam Society
Construction period 1932
Conservation award 2001

Mini Cooper has the target group of new-generation individuals which is reflected in the unique design for this showroom. Relating the concept to the idea that the display area is to look like a display box, the building has Bauhaus cubic features which achieve a distinctive boldness. The rawness and exposure of material surfaces give an industrial appearance to the building. Architectural features include a steel structure, a steel mesh, a transparent glass floor and an exposed concrete ceiling with black as the key tone to emphasise the isolated automobiles on display. Compositions of light and colour are also experimented with to add a playful character to the place.

» Science Museum 125 B

Location 928, Sukhumvit Road
Architect Sumet Jumsai Associates Co.
Owner/proprietor Department of Academic Affairs, Ministry of Education
Construction period 1982
Architectural design award 1982

The building functions as a museum and science teaching centre for children who visit on a yearly basis. It is conceived as a "technological gadget". The "gadget" itself is designed to be full of fun, as if people are visiting a shopping centre. Thus, visitors have a view of the back of the building where storage, workshops, science laboratories, design and silk-screen studios and offices are located. This is to allow visitors to fully understand and gain more interest in science. At the front of the building is a park which is used for open air exhibitions and a recreation area for the public.

» H1 126 B

Location 998/3 Soi Sukhumvit 55 (Soi Thong Lor)
Architect/designer DBALP
Proprietor Pornsak Rattanamethanon/ Orizzonte Co., Ltd.
Architectural design award 2006

The design for H1 is based on the presence of the trees. Here, the architects are interested in how to organise the simple language of modern architecture on a limited site area within a tight budget and construction schedule. Another aim is to maintain coherence to the beautiful urban fabric. The typology of a single-to double-storey building providing immediate pedestrian access was subsequently proposed. Large trees are carefully preserved in the internal courtyard; some even run through the building to illustrate the domination of nature throughout the project. The architectural

language of the steel structure is drawn upon since this offered a rapid construction method. The intricate project was completed with carefully articulated proportions, an interplay of solids and voids and an ultra thin roof overhang.

« Bangkok University Admission and Information Centre 127 B

Location Rama IV Road, Khlong Toei
Architect/designer Office AT Co., Ltd.
Owner/proprietor Bangkok University
Construction period 2007
Architectural design award 2008

Bangkok University Admission and Information Centre is a mixed-used building. The three main programmes are the admission and information centre, the student lounge and the restaurant. Therefore, an important aspect to be considered in the design was how to access each programme. In order for the building to be visible from a distance and keep the existing entrance of the campus, it is set back from the street. The main exterior stair and reflected pool are provided to link the plaza in front of the building with the admission and information centre and the student lounge. The main interior stair is linked to each programme inside the building. A black granite reflecting pool is located in front of the building to infuse the building with a refined sense of tranquillity.

» Plai Noen Pavilion 128 B

Location 1160 Rama IV Rd, Khlong Toei
Architect/designer Prince Krommaphraya Narisaranuwattiwong
Owner Mom Chao Emchit Chitraphong
Construction period 1914
Conservation award 1982

Tamnak Plai Noen (Plai Noen Pavilion) was formerly the tranquil residence of Prince Krommaphraya Narisaranuwattiwong. The pavilion was built in 1914 and comprises traditional Thai houses bought and laid out according to the Prince's design. The houses were thus built on an east-west axis in order to obtain better ventilation, rather than grouping them around a deck, as was traditionally the case. The Prince had two houses as his private quarters, one of which was a reception hall, the other a residential one. In 1964, seventeen years after the Prince passed away, a major development of the whole area was carried out. Only the Prince's two private houses were conserved, relocated and restored, with some alterations made to the materials. The houses currently serve as exhibition halls for the Prince's art objects.

» Bangkok University International College and Art Gallery

129 B

Location Rama IV Road, Khlong Toei
Architect/designer Office AT Co., Ltd. and Architects & Associates Co., Ltd.
Owner/proprietor Bangkok University
Construction period 2006
Architectural design award 2008

The International College and Art Gallery of Bangkok University is designed to be consistent with its surroundings. Space has been carved out in the volume on the first floor along the axis to create a new entrance. There is also an opening which penetrates through the building to mark a visual connection between the second and third floors – a new flexible space which can respond to new activities. This space looks like a staircase and can be used as a circulation area or as a spot to install art pieces. The building uses a variety of materials: most of the exterior walls of the art gallery are comprised of exposed precast concrete panels. The sixth storey is clad in frosted glass.

Muang Thai Phatra Complex 130 B

Location 252 Soi Udomsuk, Ratchadapisek Road
Architects Architects 49 Limited
Owner Muang Thai Insurance Company
Construction period 1988
Architectural design award 1989

The design concept behind Muang Thai Phatra Complex is to strengthen the company's identity while balancing the relationship between old and new architecture, taking into account aspects such as utilities, forms, materials and colours. The design for the project draws on its natural setting which is reflected in the elevated lobby on the second level (at a height of 12 m) and a central courtyard. This provides for an eye-catching setting amidst the bustling atmosphere of urban life. As for energy efficiency, the perimeter is wide enough to allow natural sunlight to enter the interior. The glass curtain walls and solid mass prevent heat building up and filter direct sunlight. The glass material enhances the modern appearance conveyed by the complex and contributes towards its commanding presence.

⩔ Television Broadcasting Studio and MCOT Office 131 B

Location Asok-Dindaeng Road
Architect/designer Design 103 Limited
Owner Mass Communication Organization of Thailand Public Co., Ltd.
Construction period 1980
Architectural design award 1982

Trees are carefully arranged in the front courtyard to provide the building with an abundance of shade. Parking spaces are divided into two parts to facilitate access for loading trucks. The studio is designed to be taller than the MCOT office in order to prevent direct sunlight penetrating the broadcast room and to reduce the air conditioning consumption in the buildings. Studios have also been set up outside of the station to enable shooting in front of realistic backdrops, while allowing the camera to capture a wild variety of scenes. Studios are connected by a shared pathway which is easy to access and designed so as to save electrical wiring storage space. The transmission control room is able to oversee the broadcast rooms which are located at the back to prevent the reflection of light.

⩔ Casa Optimism (Baan Khun Orapin Hemvijitraphan) 132 B

Location 4/389 Moo 6 Soi Nakniwas 37, Lat Phrao Road, Lat Phrao
Architect Boon Design
Owner/proprietor Orapin Hemvijitrapan
Construction period 2004
Architectural design award 2010

The concept behind the house is to combine the *actual* space with a *sense* of space by extracting architectural elements. The building has an open floor plan which is marked by the absence of a central column. The second-storey load-bearing walls carry the weight that rests above them. Screens made of bamboo panels have been mounted on to a metal frame, while casement windows are used as structural walls and provide an attractive finish. The building has an elevated ground level and is set back from the street, thus separating living areas from the driveway and enhancing views across the landscape. Trees are planted sporadically to provide shade. The rusty colour gives a bark-like texture to the casement windows, enabling the building to blend seamlessly into its environment.

« ACB Furniture Workshop (Aumnajchaiyakij Interior Co., Ltd.) 133 B

Location 208 Soi Lad Phrao 101, Lad Phrao Road, Bang Kapi
Architect/designer Sujin Osatarayakul Architects Co., Ltd
Owner Aumnajchaiyakij Interior Co., Ltd.
Architectural design award 2008

ACB Furniture Workshop is an industrial building amidst a tropical setting with a breathing wall system – a typical feature of traditional Thai housing. It presents a combination of two types of concrete block: the light-hole blocks enable natural light to consistently flood the interior without the use of electrical devices (appropriate for the inspection of products) while the air-hole blocks allow air flow inside the building to create comfortable working conditions. The western façade has a cantilevered roof overhang and frosted glass windows (designed for cross-ventilation) to protect the interior from the harsh glare of the tropical sun.

≈ SCG Experience 134 B

Location 1444 Praditmanutham Rd, Klongchan, Bang Kapi
Architect/designer Architects 49 Limited
Owner SCG Distribution Co., Ltd.
Construction period 2008
Architectural design award 2010

Siam Cement Group aims to build a retail channel providing knowledge and technology to students. The building reflects the company's core activity as a manufacturer of concrete materials by using precast concrete panels for the floor, roof and building envelope. For the design of the building, straight and diagonal lines form a hexagonal shape to symbolise the company's striking logo. The company aims to help reduce energy consumption and global warming by installing solar panels on the roof of the carpark as an alternative power supply. A skylight and curtain wall let natural light enter the building to create different ambiences, depending on the quality of light during the day. The entrance is decorated with green façades to produce oxygen, while a reflecting pool makes the building more inviting in appearance.

≈ 4C House 135 B

Location Nakniwas Road 20
Architect/designer Srisak Phattanawasin
Owner/proprietor Chalotorn Phaewsuwan
Construction period 2007
Architectural design award 2008

The main concept here was to create an environment in a high-density urban area with the insertion of four courtyards, rather than only providing an entire open space. Each of the courtyards is of differing size and serves a different purpose; one contains a fish pond, for example, and another a garden. Striking a balance between the small site area on offer and the demand for maximum utilisation of the area, the shape of the house embraces each open courtyard indentified sequentially by a cement-polished transverse plane perpendicular to a white-painted plane. This spatial configuration establishes a meaningful relationship between the duality posed by the indoors and outdoors.

5

≫ New Look – New Life Townhouse

136 B

Location 31-31/2 Lad Phrao Road 136 Sub-soi 1, Bangkapi
Architect/designer Vittvat Chroenpong
Owner Apichart Charoenpiwatpong
Architectural design award 2008

The existing structures are of a post-modernist design with classic Western influences, which is particularly demonstrated by the front façade. This approach was affected by limitations posed by the structural design. Coupled with the tropical climate of Thailand, the results was an accumulation of dirt and dust, making maintenance difficult. The challenge here was to use contemporary design and construction methods to achieve a harmony between the local tropical climate and the specific needs of the owners. The architectural image of the renovated building is a marriage between old and new designs, while keeping alterations to the building structure at a bare minimum – therefore saving money but maintaining a sound building structure. The stair, portico, balcony, windows and entrance have all remained in the same position. However, their dimensions may have been altered to better conform to the awning and brown faux wood siding, allowing the balcony to blend in with its surroundings. The overall composition achieves a balance between old and new architecture by combining the warmth and comfort of everyday living.

Khun Prasert Satientirakul House 137 B

Location 31 Soi 43/1 Ramkamhaeng Road
Architect Boon Design
Owner/proprietor Prasert Satientirakul
Construction period 2005
Architectural design award 2010

The design concept behind the building responds to both the tropical climate of the location and the modern lifestyle favoured by the owners. The house is slightly elevated above ground level to prevent termites and ground moisture moving up to the house. This also helps to provide a space for air conditioning compressors and mechanical systems. The open spaces are connected by a terracotta tiled roof. The wooden frame of the building is topped with a double-roof system with a wide overhang to prevent humidity and retain a balance between open spaces and living areas. Decorative columns are used to define open spaces and serve as lightweight load-bearing structures. This type of structure commonly uses plasterwork. A frame structure and prefabricated flooring were employed to reduce the construction time and materials.

Community Organizations Development Institute 138 B

Location 912 Navamin Road, Klongchan, Bang Kapi
Architect Arsom Silp Institute of the Arts, Plan Architects Co., Ltd.
Owner Community Organizations Development Institution
Construction period 2007
Architectural design award 2010

Community Organizations Development Institute is accommodated in a contemporary office building that responds to its surroundings: namely, a low-density residential area set amidst tropical settings. Therefore, the site layout has a layered appearance, with low buildings at the front set back from the street gradually increasing in height the greater the distance. The building, blending seamlessly into its environment, has an elevated ground floor, wooden walls, awning windows and a shed roof. The most important element of the building is the communal area, where consulting services and cultural exchange programmes are provided for the benefit of the community. This also serves as a recreational space for staff to mingle and exchange news.

Index of Buildings

Digits indicate the page number

Index of Architects and Firms

Digits indicate the page number

Architects

Architectural Firms and Institutions

Notes and Credits

Editor's Note

Bangkok is one of the world's most well-known tourist destinations. Travellers are fascinated by its art and cultural diversity, as well as its colourful street life which is linked to attractions such as dining, shopping and sightseeing. The city's skyline is shaped by a wide range of architectural styles evident in palaces, temples, historic buildings and modern skyscrapers.

In spite of the fact that these edifices represent the architecture of different eras, they co-exist harmoniously and, at the same time, add spice to a visit to Bangkok. However, up to now these have never been well documented in any guide-books. This book is a map-based guide to notable architecture which has been the recipient of architectural design awards by the Association of Siamese Architects under Royal Patronage (ASA).

All buildings are listed geographically within the areas and neighbourhoods which readers may wish to visit, regardless of the historic period in which they were built. Whether you are a citizen of Bangkok or a visitor with a limited amount of time on your hands, you will find this guide to be a true travel companion which takes you on an unforgettable journey for exploring what the city has to offer.

Dr. Pattaranan Takkanon,
Assistant Professor, Faculty of Architecture, Kasetsart University, Bangkok

Photo Credits

t=top
c=centre
b=bottom
l=left
r=right

Architects 49 Ltd: 140, 159l, 161l; **Architects and Associates Co., Ltd:** 136; **Arsom Silp Institute of Arts:** 163; **Duangrit Bunnage Architect Limited:** 155t; **Hemvijitraphan, Boonlert:** 159r, 162t; **Nond-Truengjaj Architects, Planners Co., Ltd:** 67; **Office AT Co., Ltd:** 156-157, 157b; **Office of Bangkok Architects Co., Ltd:** 152-153; **Pattannawasin, Srisak:** 161r; **Plan Architect Co. Ltd:** 26b, 89t, 134, 135; **Rattanawiwatpong, Napassai:** 162b; **Rungaree, Somluk:** 6-7, 93b, 103t, 106-107, 110, 111, 141, 148, 151b, 158; **Senglaung, Direk:** 37t; **Sujin Osatarayakul Architects Co., Ltd:** 160; **Teerapongramkul, Leenavat:** 62t, 66, 116-117, 138; **Trakulvech, Salila:** 115t, 118; **Winyarat, Teera and Sawitee Ananrattansuk:** 16, 17, 18-19, 20-21, 20b, 22, 23, 24-25, 26-27t, 28-29, 30, 31, 32, 33, 34-35, 35b, 36, 37b, 38-39, 40-41, 41b, 42b, 43, 44-45, 46, 47, 48, 49, 50, 51, 52-53, 60b, 60-61, 62-63, 64, 65, 68-69, 69b, 70, 71, 78-79, 79b, 80t, 80-81, 82t, 82, 83, 84-85, 85b, 86t, 86-87, 88, 89b, 90t, 90-91, 92, 93t, 100-101, 101b, 102-103, 102t, 104, 105, 106t, 107t, 108-109, 109b, 113b, 112-113, 114t, 114-115, 119, 120, 121, 122, 123, 124-125, 126, 127, 128, 129, 130, 131, 132, 133, 137, 139, 149, 150-151, 157c; **istock/ aluxum:** 5cr, 5b, 98-99; 146-147; **Chanwit Ohm:** 8-9; **Exso Minute:** 5tl, 14-15; **fototrav:** 5tr, 58-59; **Mhom:** 5cl, 76-77.

The *Deutsche Nationalbibliothek* lists this publication in the *Deutsche Nationalbibliografie*; detailed bibliographic data are available at http://dnb.d-nb.de.

ISBN 978-3-86922-358-2

Editor-in-Chief
Pattaranan Takkanon

Copyediting
Somchai Leelittam
Lersak Niyomthai
Sumet Titareyakul
Salila Trakulvech
Thanaporn Wongdontri
Arunch Sawasronnapak

Design
Sarah Zahradnik

Final Artwork
Lupe Bezzina

Maps
Katrin Soschinski

Printing
Tiger Printing (Hong Kong) Co. Ltd.
www.tigerprinting.hk

DOM publishers

asa สมาคมสถาปนิกสยาม ในพระบรมราชูปถัมภ์
The Association of Siamese Architects under Royal Patronage